EX LIBRIS

GH

· NEW ZEALAND · POHUTUKAWA

For many generations, Maori and Pakeha have loved and honoured the scarlet blossoms of the pohutukawa, the Christmas tree of Aotearoa. Of all this country's great native trees, it is perhaps the best known and the most fascinating.

Maori tradition holds the pohutukawa in special regard. The tree is said to have welcomed the Arawa canoe of the Great Fleet, and few do not know of the famous pohutukawa at Cape Reinga (the 'flowers of spirits' flight') where the souls of the dead depart for the hereafter. Pohutukawa were growing nearby when Samuel Marsden held New Zealand's first Christmas service in the Bay of Islands and, in later years, the tree's red flowers reminded homesick pioneers of the festive holly of distant Britain.

Poets and artists of both races have paid homage to the pohutukawa's magic, but *New Zealand Pohutukawa* is the first book devoted entirely to this special tree. As author and artist, brothers Geoff and Maurice Conly have combined their talents in a unique and beautiful tribute to the pohutukawa. This lovely volume will bring lasting pleasure to New Zealanders everywhere who have seen the 'flowering flame' of pohutukawa against a summer sea.

Pohutukawa trees on the rugged coastline of Mayor Island in the Bay of Plenty.

· NEW ZEALAND ·
POHUTUKAWA

Geoff & Maurice Conly

Grantham House
New Zealand

Acknowledgements

Many people who helped with the research for this book are named in the text. Their help is appreciated.

Thanks are also due to: Dr Elizabeth Edgar, of DSIR, Lincoln, for the translation of Daniel Solander's description of the pohutukawa; Mr J. P. Allen, Conservation Officer, Hauraki Gulf; Mr Ashley Cunningham of Bay View, for pointing the author in the right direction and specifically to the research of Mr S. W. Burstall, which in turn led to *Great Trees of New Zealand* by Burstall and E. V. Sale, for which copyright clearance is appreciated.

Copyright clearance is also appreciated from Miss Zillah Castle, Wellington, for permission to reprint the poem *In December* by her late brother, Ronald Castle; Mrs Barbara Hulse, Cambridge, for her poem *Nova Zelandiae*, and Mr K. A. Forsman, Auckland, for permission to use *A Pohutukawa Carol* by his late brother, Father E. A. Forsman.

The Alexander Turnbull Library gave generous advice on reference sources, as did the reference section of the Napier Public Library and the rich little library maintained by the Hawke's Bay Art Gallery and Museum.

The quest for illustrations was eased by the curator of pictorial collections at the Alexander Turnbull Library, Ms M. F. Minson, Mr Roger Blackley, curator of historical New Zealand Art at the Auckland Art Gallery, Mr Martin O'Connor and the British Museum.

Photographic help is acknowledged from Messrs David Conway (Gisborne), Les Nash, Guy Natusch, Owen Somerset Smith, all of Napier, and Neville Peat of Dunedin.

All paintings unless otherwise acknowledged by Maurice Conly.

First Published 1988

GRANTHAM HOUSE PUBLISHING

P.O. Box 17-256
Wellington 5
New Zealand

(A3) © 1988 D. Geoffrey Conly, R. Maurice Conly

ISBN 1 86934 016 7

Edited by Anna Rogers
Typeset by Wordset Enterprises Limited, Wellington
Designed by Graham Stewart of Bookprint Consultants
Printed by Kings Time Printing Press of Hong Kong in
association with Bookprint Consultants Limited, Wellington

CONTENTS

1
In the Beginning

New Zealand is a colourful land. Even the arid tan of a tussocky Central Otago or the monochrome pasture of a Hawke's Bay summer drought has a photogenic appeal. Colour at its extreme crowds the skies in the ravishing splendour of those exceptional sunsets which favour the east coast, right down to Stewart Island, otherwise known as Rakiura, land of the glowing skies. Add to these the sparkling blue of the seas off East Cape, the golden-white sands of Northland beaches, the snow-capped mountains of the scenic south, the misty blue of a rain-washed Fiordland. Even the steam drifts from a bubbling thermal bore have colour of their own — indeed, all the colours of the spectrum when sunlight sparkles through the spray.

Is it not surprising that, with so much colour decorating the New Zealand landscape, the natural vegetation is so placid — of a brownish shade (in groundcover plants) or of various orders of green? The latter, of course, prevails in the forests, where totara, kauri, matai, rimu and their fellows tower over ferns. A few trees have blossoms to provide seasonal contrast, but the evergreen, which occasionally burnishes brown in autumn, is the natural colour of the New Zealand bush.

It was not the pioneering botanists nor the explorers as such but the curious traveller-authors who noted this identifying aspect of the New Zealand flora. Ferdinand Ritter von Hochstetter, a geologist from Austria, spent nine well-ordered months in New Zealand in 1859 at the request of the government, reporting on the physical geography, natural history and geology of the country. He also dwelt on what he thought an oddity of the New Zealand bush, in that its interior was:

> . . . gloomy, everything as silent as the grave; neither gay blossoms nor gaudy butterflies and birds greet the eye or relieve the melancholy monotony of the scenery; all animal life seems extinct and, however much the curious traveller may have yearned after sylvan beauty, it is with feelings of delight that after days of tedious plodding through the dreary solitude of these gloomy and desolate woods he hails once more the cheering delight of the open landscape.[1]

Pohutukawa trees on the foreshore of Coopers Beach in Doubtless Bay, a favourite holiday
and picnic spot in Northland.

Hochstetter may have been a prejudiced commentator, having reached the security of open spaces only after 'impenetrable thickets' of forest, which had to be cut through with knife or sword at every step. It was, after all, 'untrodden wilderness' and some latter-day adventurers may envy this Austrian his virgin bush expeditions.

Hochstetter was not alone in his forest musings. Surgeon Major Arthur S. Thomson of the 58th Regiment (and how many surgeons, naval and military, found comfort in describing the New Zealand flora?) reported the New Zealand landscape as 'not soft or gay but grand and sombre. It presents to the eye a dark green colour and . . . little that is striking'.[2] Yet the major found the charm of New Zealand forests indescribable for the lovers of nature, while the 'profound silence inside the forest produced a pleasing gloom on the mind'. He found 'a society in trees' which men missed in the vast plains of fern and flax, but there was consolation, too, at Christmas in the scarlet flowers of the pohutukawa, at that season 'the most gaudy of forest trees'.[3]

The pohutukawa's Christmastide flowering, mostly in coastal isolation, was all the more emphatic, compared with the denseness of bush greenery. In the 'woods', as Hochstetter noted, 'there are scarcely any gay flowers and blossoms.'[4]

It is a fact — our flora lacks showy flowers. Most, such as the seaside ngaio or the graceful lacebark, are white and do not flaunt themselves. But count the exceptions! — the golden kowhai, the ever-abundant pink and white manuka and, of course, the rata and the pohutukawa, the red globules of the white pine (kahikatea), the tallest tree in New Zealand, or the deep reddish flowers of the puriri.

Small wonder that our poets have in the main rejected the 'sombre forests' in favour of the few more conspicuous flowering trees, such as the rata and pohutukawa. Eileen Duggan, a genuine New Zealand poet with a lyrical gift, could acknowledge that,

> . . . our flowers are pale,
> and mark of pander bees,
> Save these red trees that put forth such a blaze,
> The very Tasman could not put it out
> When summer strikes the tender of their brows.[5]

Of the rata, first cousin of the pohutukawa and mostly a southern resident, a plant of the forest which can climb the tallest tree, she wrote:

> Flowers that with one scarlet gleam
> Cover a hundred leagues, and seem
> to set the hills on fire.[6]

While admiring these red blossoms, even Ernst Dieffenbach could agree that the forest forms are 'the most beautiful in nature'. What, for instance, he asked, 'can be more delicate than the graceful rimu-pine with pendant branches or the tree ferns and stately palms', or 'the venerable rata often measuring 40 ft in circumference, and covered with scarlet flowers'?[7] (That he mentioned the rata rather than the pohutu-kawa overlooks the critics who see the rata as a parasite, devouring its host tree in a live-or-die struggle.)

But let us now turn to the pohutukawa — a gnarled, Christmastide tree illuminating many a coastal solitude, a scarlet blaze of seasonal glory, isolated from the mass of interior forest, a tree to welcome the ocean adventurer, a tree of mythology and legend, a tree of fate.

The pohutukawa was the first tree admired by the adventurers of one canoe in the Great Fleet of Maori tradition (though for the wrong reason!) and, according to Maori mythology, is the last tree seen by the souls of the departed before they leave for the mysteries of the hereafter. It was a pohutukawa, too, which watched over the first Christian service conducted in New Zealand by the missionary leader, the Rev. Samuel Marsden.

It is, by natural habitat, a North Island tree, and a tree of the northern two-thirds of the island at that. And, with the conspicuous exception of the thermal lakes, it is a tree which clings to the coast, a neighbour of beach and salt sea, an evergreen which, with its fellows in a grove in full bloom, stops 'the sun like giant red umbrellas'.[8]

Its only flamboyant rival, the kowhai, has never entered Kiwi folklore in the same way, though 'red and gold' can be admired as friendly rivals. The pohutukawa claimed a precedence if for no other reason than that it was the immediate stand-in for the holly the settlers had left behind in England.

Here was the new flower of the new land, fortuitously blossoming at the very season when pioneers' thoughts turned to the people, places and customs they had known and loved on the other side of the world. So sprays of the pohutukawa's leaves and flowers decorated the interiors of churches at Christmas, were added to Christmas dinner table decorations, blazed in a wall vase or brightened the woolshed rafters for the Christmas dance — much as happened with holly in the old country.

If legend is correct, the pohutukawa 'holly' favoured by these early settlers was born of disaster and death long ago. For once a warrior called Tawhaki visited the heavens either in search of his grandmother or to secure the services of the dog bands of Tama-i-waho to assist him in avenging his father's death. (The choice depends on which authority one listens to.)

In the latter version, Tawhaki finds the dog bands in the uppermost heaven. That chronicler of Maoridom, Elsdon Best, tells what happened in his *Maori Religion and Mythology*:

> Tawhiki persisted and, in the uppermost heaven, he found the dog bands of Tama. But Tama was a being possessed of great powers and he caused Tawhaki to fall from the uppermost heaven and so perish at the far off place where the sky hangs down. When people of this world awoke the next morning they saw that the blossoms of the rata, pohutukawa and kowhai trees were of a strange new colour produced by the blood of Tawhaki when he fell from the heavens, and that gleaming red colour they have retained from that time down to our own, the folk who now wander athwart the body of Papa, the Earth Mother.[9]

Before 19th-century Pakeha settlement, New Zealand belonged to the Maori, for a period of perhaps 1000 years, depending on whose interpretation of mythology and carbon dating and the other techniques of anthropology one accepts. Within that period the Maori from far-off Hawaiki (the 'homeland') had adapted to the new-found scene and climate in Aotearoa, had their cultivations, their pa, their tribal delineations. They chased the giant moa to extinction, fished where Maui had dropped his line, made friends with the flora and trapped and ate the fauna. They made the land their home.

Yet the process of adaptation called for readjustment, new values, new under-standings, as was emphasised on the very first landing of the Arawa canoe in the Bay of Islands. The progenitor of a tribe of fighting warriors who rejoiced in their pride of achievement as well as in their ancestry, the Arawa canoe, at its landing, faced its own moment of truth.

The chief Tauninihi was a member of the Arawa canoe and, even after the exhaust-ing voyage across the unknown seas from Hawaiki, proudly wore a red headdress of fine feathers, like the helmet of a doge and known as kura. (Kura is also a Maori word for red.) But what bordered the shoreline of this new South Pacific land which was to become New Zealand? Nothing less than a whole parade of kura; in fact, the red blossoms of the pohutukawa.

'Ah,' said Tauninihi, 'there are more kura in this land than there are kura in Hawaiki; I will cast my kura into the water.'[10] (His kura was named Taiwhakeae.) The voyagers made land, to find, to Tauninihi's chagrin, that the kura on the coast were pretty flowers, fragile and fated as blossoms are, captivating floral will o' the wisps compared with the red feathers of the parakeets of Hawaiki.

(Oddly enough, although there is a tradition of wearing red headdresses in other parts of the Pacific, the practice never extended to New Zealand although red feathers were at hand. Was there a rejection because of Tauninihi's disappointment?)

Tauninihi's headdress, washed ashore on a beach not far from where it was cast adrift, was found by a man named Mahina. And Mahina refused to give it up when approached by the original owner, saying it was the drift kura found by Mahina. Hence a traditional saying in Maoridom, 'te kura pae a Mahina' (the drift kura of Mahina), which can be broadly interpreted as, 'Finders' keepers'.[11] As the missionary printer William Colenso noted, this became a popular proverb used by those seeking to claim as their own what they happened across. The claim was usually allowed. But, added Colenso, 'no doubt there is a far deeper meaning to this ancient story than what appears on its surface.'[12]

This tale provides botanical authority for the time of year the Arawa canoe made its New Zealand landfall, for the pohutukawa blooms at Christmas. All sorts of deductions follow, from navigation by the stars across the wide Pacific to the currents which wash the ocean; seasonal weather and the exposure to which the travellers were subject in their canoes; and much else besides, not least the omens which father any great expedition.

On the voyage of the Great Fleet across the Pacific, a supernatural death threat was also avoided. Waiting unheralded on the journey was the pool known as the Throat of the Parata, a giant whirlpool into which the Arawa canoe was driven by adverse winds conjured up by an offended priest. Death hovered. The canoe commander, Ngataoroi-rangi, was equal to the challenge and sang a powerful incantation which concluded:

Eke, eke	She lifts, she ascends,
Eke panu ku!	She glides into safety!
Hui e —	O unity —
Taike e —.	O victory —.[13]

These words have been used down the generations by the descendants of the canoe to welcome their visitors.

Another version of the kura incident says it happened to the Aotea canoe. Sir George Grey, one-time Governor of New Zealand, Prime Minister and keen collector of legends of the Maori, was told the mistake took place off South Taranaki, an unlikely habitat of the pohutukawa at that time.

An interpreter compounded this error by expanding four words of the Maori text into 27 words:

Ke whiua te hutukawa	They foolishly threw away the red ornaments they wore on their heads
(The hutukawa was thrown away)	(named pohutukawa) into the sea, these being old, dirty and faded, from length of wear . . .[14]

In time, the pohutukawa became part of Maoridom, sometimes a tapu tree, a decorative tree sufficiently admired to be transplanted to regions where it was not native. It was also a recognised source of nectar for birds and hence a bait to help catch the tui and bellbird. The fowler used a peculiar cry to attract the birds to the flowers, then pulled tight on a running noose to trap the birds' legs. The medicinal qualities of the tree were recognised too; the juice of the inner bark was used to allay inflammation and to promote the healing of gunshot and gangrenous wounds, while toothache could be relieved by sucking a slice of the inner bark.

European settlers who followed the trail-breaking traders, vagabonds and explorers of the early 19th century brought new ways, new concepts, a new language, new traditions — and a new God.

Let us pause on a Bay of Islands beach on Christmas Day 1814 where the priest Samuel Marsden stands before his congregation of local Maori and the crew of the brig *Active* in an open-air church created for the occasion. 'An area of about half an acre was enclosed for the church, the roof whereof was the blue sky above, and the walls the greenfields and the bush, the golden sands and the restless ocean.' So wrote that prolific and kindly author, A. H. Reed, in *First New Zealand Christmasses 1769–1814*.

He continued: 'and on the shore the New Zealand Christmas Tree, the pohutukawa, whose scarlet flowers outshine even the glory of the English holly.'[15]

On Oihi beach Marsden himself had arranged the seating from the bottoms of old canoes and created a reading desk and pulpit, against both part of a canoe. On the highest hill in the village, a flagstaff bore the flag which Marsden saw as 'the signal and the dawn of civilisation, liberty and religion in that dark and benighted land'.[16] The worlds had met, the European and the Polynesian, this time in the presence of the European's God.

Was there literary licence in Reed's description of pohutukawa on the fringe of this 1814 beach? We know the Maori claimed whatever easily worked land was at hand for their cultivations. And then there was the notorious Bay of Islands' licentiousness, where wood (especially wood which burnt well) was as much prey to man's failings as any old-world morality. Could the pohutukawa trees have withstood such onslaughts?

Bay of Islands historian Jack Lee says, 'There is no doubt that there were pohutukawa on the cliffs on each side of the Oihi beach. They are there now, and there is no reason to believe they were not then.' A few old trees still stand on the ridgetop, near the summit of the pa.

So the pohutukawa trees survive, along with the records of that historic service when the Gospel was introduced to New Zealand, to the singing of the 'Old Hundredth' and the words of Marsden's message: 'Behold, I bring you glad tidings of great joy.'[18] The spot from which the Rev. Samuel Marsden preached that Christmas Day is identified now by the Marsden Cross, slightly more than 6 metres high — and overlooked, of course, by the pohutukawa.

In time, the European settlers came to accept the pohutukawa as a valuable tree, though probably not to the same extent as the Maori for whom the tree was part of their mythology and legend. The first Pakeha visitors treasured the giant kauri for the magnificent spars it made and a rich trade sprang from its export. In later times, the tree gained an added value from the recovery of its gum deposits.

The Maori, by comparison, worshipped the magnificent totara, the sacred child of the forest god to which great chiefs and warriors were likened and the wood of which was reserved for such special purposes as the construction of war canoes and meeting houses. They knew and respected other species, of course, and individual trees, whatever their type, were often given a tapu or reserved designation because of their situation or association. Thus there are groves of pohutukawa made tapu because they mark the site of age-old but never-forgotten battles, while other pohutukawa trees are honoured as sacred because they were resting places of the spirits of the dead on their journey north to the most famous pohutukawa of them all, that which stands at Cape Reinga, lone sentinel guarding the entrance to the underworld. Its blossoms, the crimson flowers of many stamens borne on terminal cymes, are known at Te Reinga as Te Pua o te Reinga — the flowers of spirits' flight.

By contrast, Europeans respected the pohutukawa, apart from its decorative appeal, because of its useful properties in a Pakeha way of life. Where the Maori valued the

Emily Cumming Harris (1837?–1925) *Metrosideros tomentosa (pohutukawa)* [189–?].
Watercolour, 37 × 26 cm. *Alexander Turnbull Library*

The tui has always found the pohutukawa an important source of nectar, so much so that
Maori fowlers used the flowers to bait the birds.

Oihi beach in the Bay of Islands and the Marsden Cross which stands where
the Rev. Samuel Marsden held his Christmas Day service in 1814.

bark for its medicinal qualities and for its effectiveness as firewood (the 'heartwood of iron' was third only to the puriri and kowhai as a producer of heat in both Maori and Pakeha reckoning), European settlers quickly found advantages in the peculiar growth habit of the pohutukawa — a comparatively short trunk with many massive, tortuous arms. This, allied with its great durability, made the wood specially attractive to the boatbuilder, a familiar figure in sparsely settled colonial New Zealand.

Joseph Banks, Captain Cook's companion botanist in 1769, was quick to recognise the boatbuilding potential of the pohutukawa's twists and turns and Colenso endorsed the utility of the wood. Moreover, from a boatbuilder's point of view, the wood had the extra appeal that it was immune to the teredo (seaworm) when exposed to salt water.

The natural bends of the pohutukawa were the massive ribs of the largest sailing ship to be built in New Zealand, the *Stirlingshire*. Laid down on Great Barrier Island in 1840, she was 106 feet (32 metres) long, 25 feet (7·5 metres) broad and had a draft of 19 feet (5·7 metres). Her 409 tons were spread over two decks, while she was carvel-planked in kauri. According to a Great Barrier Island promotional booklet, *Once upon a time in an island on the ocean*, the *Stirlingshire* was probably the first vessel of kauri construction to reach England. And, presumably, the first with pohutukawa ribs.

Botanist Thomas Kirk (and father of the former State Forest Service) was so concerned about the shipbuilding industry's consumption of pohutukawa that he argued for conservation of the Kermadec pohutukawa:

> In view of the increasing scarcity of pohutukawa in the North Island it would be far wiser to conserve the small-leaved pohutukawa of the Kermadec Islands than to allow it to be destroyed merely to facilitate settlement, which must of necessity be restricted. Nearly 200 persons are now engaged in ship and boatbuilding, of whom fully three-quarters are employed in the Auckland district, where alone pohutukawa is to be procured.[19]

Kirk recorded that during 1885, 403 boats and 53 vessels of from 50 to 200 tons burden were built in the colony, the total value of material and labour alone being estimated at £47,116. By far the greater portion of this work was performed in the Auckland district — 316 boats and 31 vessels.

Pioneer settlers used pohutukawa planks for such special purposes as machine-beds and bearings, and even for the framing and sills of dock gates. The pohutukawa also had a variety of applied uses from the decorative to the severely practical, even fulfilling such a delicate role as its red stamens being used as taste buds in cups of tea, as once described by journalist-author E. V. Sale.

With both Maori and Pakeha, too, the tree still finds a questionable role in the interpretation of seasonal weather. For instance, almost every early summer someone somewhere looks at an early-flowering pohutukawa and predictably forecasts a long dry summer and the 'news' is faithfully recorded in Press Association messages throughout the country, including those regions which know of the tree only by repute. And a late-flowering pohutukawa is interpreted as an omen of a short, wet summer.

The truth, experts say, is more likely to be found in the climatic conditions prevailing when the tree sets flower or leaf buds. A dry autumn, for example, putting a tree under stress, is likely to encourage flower buds as a defence mechanism. Again, it is contended that the pohutukawa flowers according to the previous summer's weather, a good flowering one summer being followed by a year of good seed set and fewer flowers. But it has also been said that, in districts where the pohutukawa does not occur naturally, the older the introduced tree grows, the better its flowering.

It is a long way from the present, with its pohutukawa weather 'omens' and concern for the preservation of the historic or more noble specimens, back to the beginnings, shared, in their own widely spaced timespans, by the Maori voyagers of the Great Fleet and Samuel Marsden's congregation of Christmas Day 1814.

A pohutukawa tree at its scenic best, against a typical East Coast background of white sands and blue sea.

2
Pohutukawa Pioneers

 he distinction of describing the pohutukawa and many more of New Zealand's botanical riches to the world fell to two botanists of great distinction, Joseph Banks and Daniel Solander, scientists who were of the ship's company of HMS *Endeavour* commanded by the newly commissioned First Lieutenant James Cook on his first voyage to the Pacific in 1769.

Captain Cook's name lives in history as the officer who claimed New Zealand for the British Crown, by raising the British flag at Mercury Bay and cutting the date (13 November 1769) and the ship's name on a tree near the spot used for watering the vessel. His name is honoured as an eminent leader in ocean exploration.

He was selected by the Admiralty to observe the transit of Venus from some Pacific base (he chose Tahiti) and then to try to locate the great southern continent (*Terra australis incognita*), which was reputed to balance in the Southern Hemisphere the great land masses which dominate the northern half of the globe. He did not find the continent because it was not there, but he followed additional Admiralty instructions and sailed on to New Zealand, there to chart, with extraordinary accuracy considering his means, the coastline, and to lead the scientists aboard his ship in prosecuting 'the design of making discoveries'[1] in the South Seas.

Of the 'discoveries' that concerned New Zealand, flora must be counted of great significance. The efforts of Banks, Solander and the watercolour artist Sydney Parkinson resulted in the introduction to the botanical world of descriptions and illustrations of distinctive New Zealand plants. Not least among them was the 'Pohutuiawha'.

The Maori knew and respected the pohutukawa ('ironwood') but this tree, along with 300 or 400 other indigenous plants, was completely unknown to other than the native inhabitants of New Zealand. That this was little more than 200 years ago confirms how relatively quickly a rarity can become a commonplace, marvellous though it remains.

So, while the primary purpose of the voyage was satisfactorily achieved, in observing the transit of Venus, there were extraordinary unexpected dividends in Cook's

An historic first-a pohutukawa sprig as depicted by Sydney Parkinson, artist during Captain Cook's first visit to New Zealand. *Courtesy British Museum (Natural History)*

voyage, such as the annexation of New Zealand, the mapping of its coastline, the observation of the transit of the planet Mercury (at Mercury Bay on 9 November), an account of the Maori people — and the botanical achievements of Banks, Solander and party.

Of the 94 people aboard HMS *Endeavour*, 10 were civilians. One was the astronomer Green; the remainder comprised the suite led by Banks and Solander — two artists, a secretary (who was also a naturalist-artist) and four servants, who happened also to be trained collectors, in all a sizeable number for a barque of modest size.

Joseph Banks was a rich young man of 25, well educated, a fellow of the Royal Society, who could well afford to indulge his enthusiasm for botanical studies. (It was said that he financed stores and equipment and botanical costs of the *Endeavour*'s expedition to the tune of some £10,000. Knighted for his services to science, he became a long-serving president of the Royal Society, where the idea of observing the transit of Venus, and indeed the *Endeavour*'s voyage, originated.

Banks recruited as his chief assistant for the voyage Dr Daniel Solander, a Swede who had been encouraged by the celebrated Linnaeus to spread the Linnaean creed in England. He was popular. The two artists were Sydney Parkinson (commissioned to draw and paint the new plants) and Alexander Buchan (to sketch people and landscapes). In addition, Herman Diedrich Sporing, Solander's clerk at the British Museum and a natural history student, was employed to serve as Banks' and Solander's clerk in the *Endeavour*. A competent draughtsman, he was able to relieve Parkinson of part of the heavy art load, particularly when Buchan died at Tahiti on the voyage south. Parkinson died at Batavia on the homeward journey, but his impressive volume of work remains as a tribute to his skills, enterprise and energy.

Banks and Solander were with their captain when Cook first stepped ashore in New Zealand, at Turanganui (below Kaiti hill, at the present port of Gisborne), where the Cook memorial stands. This was a sorry botanical introduction for in the short time the vessel was berthed in Poverty Bay the botanists were able to collect 'not above 40 species of plants in our boxes, which is not to be wondered at, as we were so little ashore and always at the same spot'.[2] Friendly contact with the resident Maori was not possible; the Europeans fired fatal shots in the first afternoon and the next morning, and six Maori were killed within 24 hours.

Banks wrote in his journal:

I am aware that most humane men who have not experienced things of this nature will censure my conduct in firing upon people in their boat, nor do I myself think that the reason I had for seizing upon her will at all justify me; and had I thought that they would have made the least resistance I would not have come near them; but as they did, I was not to stand still and suffer either myself or those that were with me to be knocked on the head. Thus ended the most disagreeable day of my life has yet seen; black be the mark for it and heaven send that such may never return to embitter future reflections.[3]

No food, no water, unfriendly contact with the natives and a mere 40 species, well may Cook have lamented that this unfriendly coast 'afforded us no one thing we wanted'.[4] So he called the region Poverty Bay, rather than, as first considered, Endeavour Bay.

Banks and Solander went ashore to botanise whenever opportunity offered, however brief the visit. The Maori inhabitants were friendlier the farther north the *Endeavour* sailed, but the scientists were often frustrated, not least when Cook would not sail into Dusky Sound to allow further botanical field studies; the captain did not trust the offshore-onshore winds he observed.

Geographically, the Banks-Solander visit is preserved in placenames: Banks Peninsula (to the south-east of Christchurch) and Solander Island (in Foveaux Strait).

They were seasonally fortunate in visiting New Zealand in the Southern Hemisphere spring and summer, when plant life was at its flowering best. Moreover, the *Endeavour* sailed many New Zealand waters, from Tolaga Bay and the Bay of Islands to Queen Charlotte Sound and Admiralty Bay. Banks recorded their fieldwork in his journal:

October 24, 1769: Dr Solander and I went ashore, botanising off Hawke's Bay.
October 25: Went ashore this morning and renewed our search for plants, etc., with great success . . .
January 25, 1770: Dr Solander and I (who have nearly exhausted all the plants in our neighbourhood) went today to search for mosses and small things, in which we had great success, gathering several very remarkable ones.[5]

Overall, however, the botanists regretted a lack of variety in New Zealand's flora: 'Though the country is covered with an abundant verdure of grass and trees, yet I cannot say that it is productive of such great variety as many countries I have seen: the entire novelty, however, of the greater part of what we found recompensed us as natural historians for the want of variety.'[6]

Banks was a keen observer with a practical mind, ever on the alert for economic uses of the plants and trees he found. Flax (*Phormium tenax*) attracted him, obviously, while he found appeal in the yam and sweet potato as foodstuff for ships' crews. The only fruit he found he dismissed as 'a few kinds of insipid berries'.[7] But timber was very much an attraction.

First of the trees Joseph Banks listed in his journal was the pohutukawa (*Metrosideros robusta*):

The woods, however, abound in excellent timber, fit for any kind of building in size, grain and apparent durability. One, which bears a very conspicuous scarlet flower made up of many threads, and which is as big as an oak in England, has a very heavy hard wood which seems well adapted for the cogs of mill-wheels, etc., or for any purpose for which very hard wood is used . . .[8]

This was the pohutukawa introduced in the English language — 'a very conspicuous scarlet flower' and 'a very heavy hard wood'.

Daniel Solander was later to describe the pohutukawa fully in the manuscript 'Primitiae Florae Novae Zelandiae . . .' (Beginnings of a flora of New Zealand or a catalogue of plants collected in the North and South Islands between 8 October–31 March 1769–1770.) He went on to detail the growth — the branches, leaves, petioles, flower-heads, petals, filaments, ovary, capsule and seeds, the last-named 'very numerous, like golden sawdust, shining'.

But what kind of picture did this description convey to the wider botanical world? Could Solander's readers imagine a pohutukawa in Christmas flower, blossoming richly scarlet against dark green leaves, white sand, blue sea?

Alfred Sharpe (1836–1908) *Pohutukawa*, 1876.
Watercolour, 448 × 620 mm.
Collection of Auckland City Art Gallery, presented by Rear-Admiral F. Burgess-Watson, 1935

Rev. Alfred Watson Hands (1849–1927)
Pohutukawa trees. Rangitoto from North Shore, Auckland, 1887
Watercolour, 18 × 35 cm. *Alexander Turnbull Library*

Still, the message brought back to England after a voyage of two years 11 months was of an 'entire novelty' compensating for the want of variety. The voyagers landed with descriptions of 360 new plants from New Zealand (as well as much other material from other ports of call), copious notes of their observations, plant samples and a rich collection of drawings and paintings. Linnaeus described the results of their labours as:

> Their matchless and truly astonishing collection, such as have never been seen before, nor may ever be seen again . . . I have every day been figuring to myself the occupations of my pupil Solander, now putting his collection in order . . . throwing the whole into classes . . . distinguishing by new names and definitions such as formed new genera, with their species. Thus . . . the world will be delighted and benefited by all these discoveries; and the foundations of true science will be strengthened so as to endure through all generations . . .'[9]

Solander was responsible for completing the descriptions of their discoveries, Banks for supervising the completion of Parkinson's artwork, employing artists to round off incomplete sketches, drawings and paintings which Parkinson had begun and described. Banks also undertook the preparation of engraved copper plates, an immense task, threatened by Banks' desire to sail south again with Cook when the latter, now a commander, set forth from Plymouth in 1772 in command of the *Resolution*, the *Adventure* attached, in a new search for the mystic continent and other places south. Banks quarrelled over the accommodation offered his staff, deeming it sadly inadequate, and stayed ashore, concentrating on the production of the engravings. Cook sailed with other scientific staff.

Solander's work was not ended when he died in 1782. Banks went on to high honours, including a baronetcy, the presidency of the Royal Society for an extraordinary term of 42 years and the office of chief counsellor on all scientific matters to the king. He lived until 1820 but, in spite of all his efforts, did not see publication of the engravings over which he had laboured so long.

New Zealanders have yet to see all the engravings, although sets are held at the Auckland Institute and Museum, the National Museum (Wellington) and the Alexander Turnbull Library (Wellington), while a photocopy of the original 'Primitiae Florae Novae Zelandiae' is held by the National Museum and 183 plates are held by the Canterbury University Library. The manuscript is in Latin; accurate translation requires the expert services of a botanist who is a good Latinist (or a Latinist who is also a good botanist!).

Although the trustees of the British Museum agreed that the beautiful copperplate engravings commissioned by Banks could be published, it must always be regretted that these masterpieces, done with such care and accuracy, languished for years. Joseph Hooker commented: 'About 700 plates were engraved on copper, in folio, at Banks's expense and a few prints or proofs were taken, but they were never published. Five folio books of neat manuscript and the coppers rest in the hands of the trustees of the British Museum. The question arises, Why were they never utilised? . . . This has always been regarded as an insoluble problem.'[10]

Hooker, writing this in 1896, thought it was Solander's death which arrested publication, but more recent speculation suggests that Banks had run out of money, while other patrons were impossible to find because of the extraordinary cost of ensuring accurate prints from the plates. Fortunately the series has been published at last, though at a seemingly prohibitive price.

Had dreams been realised earlier, many of the plates could have been reproduced in Thomas Kirk's *The Student's Flora of New Zealand*, published posthumously by the Government Printer in 1899. This authoritative work was completed by T. F. Cheeseman, curator of the Auckland Museum, and re-issued as *Manual of New Zealand Flora*, but instead of the Banks-Solander engravings, as originally envisaged (and as authorised by the trustees), illustrations for the book were commissioned from Miss Matilda Smith, of Kew Gardens. The Kirk-Cheeseman book was published in 1905 and Miss Smith's volume of illustrations in 1914. It would have been appropriate had New Zealand undertaken the first publication of most of the plates — some few had been reprinted — as the home of the plants so meticulously introduced to the world by the country's two first botanical pioneers.

Botanical interest in New Zealand was maintained during Cook's two subsequent voyages to New Zealand, particularly on the second voyage when the *Resolution*'s complement included artist William Hodges, the Forsters (naturalist father, draughtsman son) and a late recruit, from Cape Town, the natural historian Anders Sparrman. This was a more productive botanical team than sailed on Cook's last, fatal voyage. Admiralty artist John Webber was more concerned with places and people, notably 'The Death of Cook', although this was a vicarious depiction since he was not present at the killing. Surgeon William Anderson, the sole botanical collector aboard the *Resolution*, 'collected nothing of importance', according to Hooker.[11]

Whalers, sealers, traders — and plant collectors. The Europeans abroad in New Zealand 20 years before the signing of the Treaty of Waitangi were, of necessity, venturesome souls, treading in the footsteps of Cook and his companies. Some of the newcomers sought profits, others knowledge, while a leavening of intrepid adventurers looked to new horizons purely for the joy of discovery.

Although Christianity was being preached among the Maori, the old ways often died hard, as the artist Augustus Earle found in 1827 when he recorded the presence of slaves. And this, it should be remembered, was only 160 years ago. Earle paused at the Bay of Islands to watch slaves preparing a morning repast 'in a beautiful bay, surrounded by high rocks and overhanging trees . . . .'. (The trees, given the seaside site in the Bay of Islands must, odds on, have been pohutukawa.) Earle continued:

> the chiefs sat in mute contemplation, their arms piled up in regular order on the beach. . . .
> Their richly ornamented war canoes were drawn up on the strand; some of the slaves were
> unloading stores, others were kindling fires. To me, it all seemed to realise some of the
> passages of Homer, where he describes the wanderer Ulysses and his gallant band of
> warriors. . . .[12]

Time moves on and the scene becomes history, but those pohutukawa trees which guarded the high rocks on the strand could be among those which still bloom each Christmas in salute to another year.

The Austrian geologist Ferdinand von Hochstetter in 1859 saw similar pohutukawa trees on 'the high bluffs on the Waitemata', though the trees were scattered, ' the last remains of the beautiful vegetation that once decked the shores of the harbour.' Hochstetter also approvingly reported how settlers used the 'charming purple blossoms' of this 'Christmas tree' to decorate their churches. [13]

These same settlers were busy developing their farms and communities, as Hochstetter noted:

From year to year improvements are going on; the bush dwindles away; crop succeeds crop; the log-house has been supplanted by a pleasant, commodious country-house, surrounded with blooming gardens and waving fields. Herds of well-fed cattle are grazing in the pastures; horses are skipping and plunging in the meadows; friends have settled in the neighbourhood; smooth lanes and neat paths are winding between hedges and through the woods from farm to farm. And close by the wayside stands a church; a tavern is there, and the first trading-shop too has already been opened. Where of late there stood but a scanty isolated log-house, there is now — it cannot be called a village, nor is it quite a town; it is — a fragment of a town. [14]

Claus Edward Fristrom (1864–1942) *Pohutukawa.*
Oil on cardboard, 188 × 260 mm. *Collection of Auckland City Art Gallery*

A view from Kohimarama Beach with Rangitoto in the background.

What would Hochstetter and his contemporaries say now of the building development crowding the shores of the Waitemata harbour, of the high-rise properties of downtown Auckland, of a harbour bridge dominating the skyline and leading to still more residential and business development in a region where once horses skipped in the meadows, cattle grazed in the pastures and 'the sylvan huts' were but a stepping-stone from log-house to country-house? And where now are those pohutukawa? Scattered though they were in the dying 1850s, they testified to the glories that once had been.

Augustus Earle and Ferdinand von Hochstetter were but two of a number of early botanical explorers who helped to describe the riches awaiting discovery in New Zealand. The missionary printer William Colenso (1811–99), 'the foremost botanical explorer', could be called a 'resident' botanist compared with the visitors, who came and went, though each contributed some quantum of knowledge about this southernmost land. Some are not part of the pohutukawa story, because they concentrated their attentions on southern New Zealand. A surprising number were ships' surgeons (or assistant-surgeons) who took time off from guarding seamen's health to botanise — the eminent Joseph Hooker, assistant surgeon in the *Erebus*, 1839; Ernst Dieffenbach of the ship *Tory*, 1839; Dr D. Lyall, assistant-surgeon of the *Terror*, part of the British Antarctic Expedition, 1841; and Dr E. Raoul, who visited the Bay of Islands and Banks Peninsula, 1840–41.

A pre-annexation visitor who, with his brother, became closely associated with New Zealand was Allan Cunningham, of Kew Gardens, chosen by Banks to botanise in New Zealand (in 1826 and 1838) from a Sydney base. His brother, Richard, also then living in Sydney, added to his brother's works. Allan Cunningham is credited by the noted botanist Thomas Kirk with having described the pohutukawa in detail, but too soon, in 1839, his arduous exertions on his exploration journeys led to an untimely death. He bequeathed his name as an eminent Australian botanist and explorer.

Although he spent only about three months in New Zealand, aboard the Antarctic research ship *Erebus* in 1839, Sir Joseph Hooker's contribution to New Zealand botany was considerable and his *Handbook of New Zealand Flora*, published in London in 1867, remained the standard reference work until the end of the century. His description of the pohutukawa began: 'A short, stout, much-branched tree, 30–40 feet high; branches very stout . . .'.[15]

Two 'resident' botanists created the standard reference work on New Zealand botany which succeeded Hooker's *Handbook*. Thomas Cheeseman (1846–1923), who wrote 101 scientific papers, quit farming to become secretary of the Auckland Institute in 1874 and became curator of the Auckland Museum. His botanical research took him to most parts of New Zealand — Mount Cheeseman in the Craigieburn Range in Central Otago is named after him — while he also went on expeditions offshore, to the Kermadecs, the Three Kings and the Cook Islands. Cheeseman's main memorial is his *Manual of New Zealand Flora*, published by the Government Printer in 1906, a work he took over from Thomas Kirk on the latter's death in 1898.

A keen botanist, Kirk was for some years curator and secretary of the Auckland Museum and Auckland Institute but, after a period as a lecturer in natural science, went on to become chief conservator of state forests, in which office he organised the Forestry Department. It was said of him that 'no other botanist ever acquired such a complete familiarity with the flora of New Zealand'.[16]

Kirk was impatient with the casual and often erroneous ways in which trees were described. In his preface to *The Forest Flora of New Zealand* (1889) he hoped not only to 'diffuse knowledge of the forest resources of the colony', but also to establish a uniform series of common names:

> owing to the loose manner in which common names are generally employed in the colony, timbers of but little value are frequently used instead of the kinds specified, often causing needless expenditure and great inconvenience. One instance may be mentioned here: At least a dozen kinds of small-leafed trees are termed "birch" with the prefix black, white, red, brown, grey or even yellow applied as the imagination of the bushman may suggest . . . The brown birch of Otago is the white birch of Nelson; the white birch of Westland, again, is a totally different tree; the black birch of Auckland is termed red birch in Wellington. . . .[17]

While regional interpretations and appellations may have appalled him, at least he was in no doubt of the appeal of the pohutukawa, 'perhaps the most magnificent plant in New Zealand flora':

> it [*Metrosideros tomentosa*] attains upwards of 70 ft in height, often with a comparatively short trunk and numerous large tortuous arms clothed with bold foliage, green above but white and silver beneath: from the beginning of December to the middle of January its branches are crowned from base to summit with large panicles of glittering blood-red flowers, affording a pleasing contrast with the white undersurface of the leaves as the branches are from time to time uplifted by the breeze.[18]

Kirk added a mournful note, reporting that the tree 'had been wantonly destroyed in many localities and is now very scarce in districts where it was formerly plentiful'.[19]

The quality of Thomas Kirk's work was greatly respected by Dr Leonard Cockayne (1855–1934), one of the country's more distinguished natural history leaders and botanists who enjoyed an international reputation. He was a prolific researcher and writer with more than 100 papers on botany and related subjects to his credit, as well as three or four books.

Writer Mona Gordon saw him as combining 'the patience of Cheeseman, the energy of Kirk, with something entirely his own — a parental interest in the young plant striving for maturity through varied stages of growth'.[20] His living memorial is the Otari Native Plant Museum which he established in Wellington for the cultivation of native plants in their natural surroundings.

Sarah Ann Featon (1847/48?–1927) *Metrosideros aurata, from Collinwood . . . 35.*
[ca. 1889–1926]
Watercolour, 30·2 × 24 cm. *Alexander Turnbull Library*

Emily Cumming Harris (1837?–1925) *Metrosideros tomentosa — pohutukawa.* [ca. 1880]
Watercolour, 23 × 17 cm. *Alexander Turnbull Library*

Alfred Sharpe (1836–1908) *Oyster Cove, North Head, Auckland 1879.*
Watercolour, 505 × 412 mm. *Collection of Auckland City Art Gallery,*
presented by Mr Norman B. Spencer, 1967

Another memorial is *The Trees of New Zealand*, the book he wrote in association with E. Phillips Turner and which was dedicated to Thomas Kirk, 'for more than three decades the leader of the botanical inquiry in the colony . . .'[21] The pohutukawa, of course, was listed in this volume, first as a tree which had 'its principal importance as a feature enhancing the beauty of the characteristic shoreline'.[22] But Dr Cockayne also had a very practical appreciation of the application of pohutukawa timber:

> The wood is dark red, dense, heavy, compact, and very durable. Its tortuous habit of growth makes it of value for ship-timbers and for this purpose it has been employed extensively since the early days of settlement. It is suitable for use when exposed to salt water, since it is immune to the attack of the teredo [marine worm]. Like the other species of the genus, it makes excellent firewood.[23]

So wrote one of the greatest of New Zealand botanists, certainly the leader of his era and one whom, it can be hoped, also helped to inspire another generation of botanists to explore and discover New Zealand flora.

Early New Zealand botanists may have been male but among the artists there were some competent women painters. Martha King, who arrived in New Zealand in 1840, has been described as the first resident botanical artist. Miss Matilda Smith of Kew Gardens was an absentee artist of sorts with her illustrations for the Kirk-Cheeseman book, but other artists working in New Zealand included Emily Harris (1837–1925), Georgina Hetley (published in the 1880s) and Sarah Featon, who shared with her husband Edward a keen interest in New Zealand plants. The couple's enthusiasm resulted in the publication in 1889 of *The Art Album of New Zealand Flora: Being a Systematic and Popular Description of the Native Flowering Plants of New Zealand and the Adjacent Islands*. A publishing landmark, this was the first book printed in Wellington complete with colour plates.

Edward Featon wrote the text, Sarah painted the pictures. So plate 37 shows the pohutukawa, a 'handsome and useful tree' which, among other virtues, had juice of the inner bark said to possess 'a medicinal virtue and the Maoris are accustomed to use it to allay inflammation and promote healing in gunshot and gangrenous wounds'.[24] Edward continued:

> The pohutukawa blossoms in December, when its profusion of crimson tasselled flowers imparts a beauty to the rugged coast line and sheltered bays which may fairly be called enchanting. To the settlers it is known as the "Christmas tree", and sprays of its foliage and flowers are used to decorate the interiors of churches, and dwellings during the festive Christmas-tide. The time-honoured plum-pudding is likewise garnished with its floral offering, and it serves to keep fresh in the minds of many the once loved Holly of the old land.[25]

But of all the tributes to the attractions of the pohutukawa, listen to this from the far south of New Zealand where the tree was a botanical stranger. W. Martin, a training college lecturer in nature study and sometime president of the Otago Institute, noted in *The New Zealand Nature Book* that 'some of the most handsome and striking trees in the country' prefer a purely coastal station, such as the pohutukawa. And he added:

> The pohutukawa (*Metrosideros tomentosa*) is, during midsummer, the glory of the northern coasts and of the lake margins in the thermal districts. Its massive form, gnarled branches, silvery leaves and flaming flowers combine to entitle it to a foremost place among the showiest of the world's trees. A visit to Rangitoto or the Coromandel Peninsula during the flowering season leaves a memory not soon to be forgotten.[26]

Trevor Lloyd (1863–1937) *The Christmas Tree.* [ca. 1920]
Etching. *Alexander Turnbull Library*

3
The Foremost Botanist

I n New Zealand's history, one botanist stands out — the learned missionary printer William Colenso (1811–99). Pioneer scientist, traveller extraordinary, keen correspondent, keener collector, he wrote extensively.

No less an authority than Sir Joseph Hooker praised Colenso, a far-flung agent for Kew Gardens:

> who, during many successive years, has collected throughout the whole length of the Northern Island with great care and skill, discovering more new and interesting plants (especially on the Ruahine Range, Tongariro, Hikurangi, etc.) than any botanist since Banks and Solander. In every respect Mr Colenso is the foremost New Zealand botanical explorer, and the one to whom I am most indebted for specimens and information.[1]

Not unexpectedly, Colenso was one of a handful of distinguished contributors to the first volume of the *Transactions and Proceedings of the New Zealand Institute*, published in 1868. (The editor was James Hector and contributors included Julius Haast, W. T. L. Travers, Walter Buller and Captain F. W. Hutton as well as Colenso.)

Colenso's essay, written for the New Zealand Exhibition of 1865, was entitled 'Geographic and Economic Botany of New Zealand' and began with the observation that it was very nearly a century since the botany of New Zealand first became known

Emily Cumming Harris (1837?–1925) *Pohutukawa, clematis, bluebell, snowberry and ranunculus* [1800]
Watercolour 54 × 37 cm. *Alexander Turnbull Library*

to science, thanks to Banks and Solander. He recalled:

When the writer, in January 1838, first visited those forests at "Hawahowa" (Uaua), Tolago Bay (whence the earliest specimens of fine plants peculiar to New Zealand were first obtained by those botanists), a deep reverential indescribable feeling stole over him on treading the same ground which Banks and Solander and Cook had trod, and on viewing the remarkable cliffs heightened doubtless through conversing with the few old New Zealanders still dwelling there, who have seen and recollected those patriarchs of British enterprise in New Zealand. . . .[2]

Colenso arrived in New Zealand in 1834 as catechist and printer to the Church Missionary Society, although from 1852 until near his death he was estranged from the society because of his sexual association with a Maori 'wife' at Napier. His earliest botanical collections were made between Whangarei and North Cape, a region where the pohutukawa abounded on coastal cliffs and beaches. Colenso noted this presence when, in this *Transactions* essay, he set out to answer his question, 'How does the vegetation of this Northern Island of New Zealand appear when seen for the first time?' The quick answer depended on the 'place whence the newly arrived beholder last came; and second, the place in New Zealand where he lands; not forgetting his expectations — as the eye ever sees what the mind brings.'

If he last left the shore of Great Britain, then the recollection of her verdant fields may cause the brown fern-clad hills and dark-green forests of New Zealand to appear the more gloomy and sad. If his last landscapes were either South African or Australian, then their glaucous sea-green hue and arid appearance will be agreeably contrasted with New Zealand forest vegetation; but if he should have come hither direct from the sunny skies and islands of the tropics, with their perennial light ever-green dress, then the New Zealand hills and dells may appear very sombre, and will suffer from recollection and comparison. Again, if he should happen to anchor in one of the many rivers or harbours north of the Thames, while the ubiquitous brown fern (*Pteris esculenta*) is everywhere, he will be struck with the appearance of the white mangrove (*Avicennia officinalis*) growing within the range of the tide, and the romantic pohutukawa (*Metrosideros tomentosa*) pendant from the cliffs or perched on some rocky headland. . . .[3]

Colenso went on to survey the flora of New Zealand in a far-ranging and detailed account which included paragraphs on the more significant trees under various headings — timber trees, plants of utility and ornament, and timber trees commonly split for use or chopped or sawn into short chunks (rarely into boards or planks). These included the puriri, manuka, black and red birches, aka, rata and pohutukawa.

The pohutukawa, he wrote,

is another large hard-wooded tree of diffuse irregular growth. Its habitat is the immediate sea shore of the north parts of the island; where, on rocky headlands and cliffs, sometimes pendent, it forms a striking and picturesque object. It is very robust, sometimes being 4 or even 5 feet in diameter, but the trunk and branches are invariably more or less crooked. Nevertheless it is a very valuable tree, especially for ship-building purposes, where its gnarled and crooked character make it highly serviceable for timbers, knees, breast-hooks, etc.; it is also used for making ship's blocks, and for building piles. This wood presents a very handsome grain, a rich rose colour, and a high polish when worked up by the cabinetmaker, and choice pieces are in great demand. The area, or zone, in which this valuable tree is found being very limited, its wood will soon be exhausted unless some means are speedily made use of to preserve or economize it.[4]

A reprieve of sorts came with the introduction or development of other materials, though the march of civilisation was to wreak even heavier damage along the Waitemata shorelines. To this extent Colenso's pessimism was justified. He was a man of many visions, imagining silk being produced from the mulberry plant grown in the warm climate of the northern part of the North Island, and oil from the European olive, and cochineal, cinchona and coffee, even tobacco. But he was correct in appreciating that the warm weather and rich volcanic soil north of the Thames would 'doubtless produce wine and oil in abundance',[5] as happens now near Auckland city.

Keen botanical observer that he was, Colenso was only human and may sometimes have faltered, notably when he reported having seen pohutukawa growing on the edge of Lake Waikaremoana. He was kneeling in the centre of a canoe ('a frail bark') with 'my hands on each gunwale and in the water of the lake during the whole passage' and it was a matter of natural prudence that the modest fleet of canoes which comprised the expedition should keep as close as possible to the base of 'the everlasting hills . . . so as to have them to swim to if upset'. Certainly it was not his precarious position which persuaded him that, for the first time, far away from the immediate sea coast, he saw the pohutukawa: 'It grew also in similar rocky situations close to the water's edge and after the same irregular and diffuse manner.'[6]

Colenso's interest was aroused not only by the presence of a pohutukawa in this inland setting but also by a fine *Loranthus* (mistletoe) flourishing parasitically on the tree's branches. So he had his canoe run ashore on to a little beach at the margin of the forest, to obtain some of the parasite's profusion of scarlet blossom. Obviously he was close enough to recognise the tree he had identified as a pohutukawa. But was it a pohutukawa? Perhaps a specimen transplanted by a wandering Maori for reasons best known to himself? Or was he mistaken? Elsdon Best, another authority on Maoridom, questioned Colenso's identification, on the basis of information that no local Maori knew of such a specimen on the lake shore. Could Colenso have mistaken a rock-growing rata?

To complicate a minor issue, not so far north were the inland fresh water lakes of Tarawera and Rotoiti, with their own very definite shoreline pohutukawa, some of which flourish on the latter lake to this day. But then, were there special geophysical reasons for their presence? The pohutukawa which once adorned the shore of Lake Tarawera, magnificent specimens according to contemporary accounts, were wholly destroyed in the eruption of Mount Tarawera in June 1886.

A scientific comparison of the pohutukawa timber with other New Zealand timbers and certain deciduous trees concluded Colenso's notable essay. A contraction of his tables is given here:[7]

Botanical name	Other name	Stiffness	Strength	Toughness	Weight a cubic ft	Specific gravity
Metrosideros tomentosa	Pohutukawa	126	109	94	52·2	·834
English oak (Sussex)					39·0	·625
English beech (Oxfordshire)					41·2	·658
Riga fir					37·10	·602
Ceylon teak					47·3	·755
Dammara australis	Kauri	90	99	102	25·3	·403
Podocarpus totara	Totara	49	61	57	39·5	·629
Dacrydium cupressinum	Rimu	90	81	95	34·6	·560
Vitex littoralis	Puriri	100	100	100	52·5	·837
Leptospermum scoparium	Manuka	—	—	—	57·9	·921
Metrosideros robusta	Rata	89	103	138	—	—
*Edwardsia grandiflora**	Kowhai	—	—	—	43·13	·701

The first three columns of figures were acknowledged by Colenso to the *Church Almanac* for 1847, the last two columns to W. W. Saunders' catalogue in *Report of Juries*, Exhibition 1851.

William Colenso's name is remembered today in the names of a variety of plants he discovered in New Zealand, the botanical appellation honouring a scientist, amateur though he was, who was identified as the foremost New Zealand botanical explorer of his day.

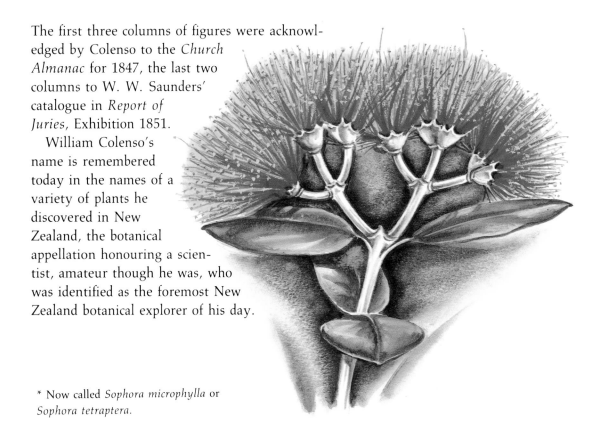

* Now called *Sophora microphylla* or *Sophora tetraptera*.

4
The Sacred and the Great

ew Zealand's historic and notable trees have been identified off and on down the years, initially somewhat haphazardly, latterly under district schemes maintained by territorial local authorities, often supported by voluntary tree societies. Registers of trees maintained under the district schemes list the selected trees under the classifications visual amenity (VA), botanic (B) and historic (H), while other entries give the species, its situation (109 Shelly Beach Road) and the relevant map reference.

'Councils appreciate the part trees play in making a place good for people to live in and, indeed, the effect mature trees have on the valuation of a property,' explains a tree society newsletter when asking if tree ordinances in fact protect trees. 'They [councils] all claim they want to protect notable trees, trees that are landmarks, trees on coastline, trees that are botanically interesting. And they are no doubt sincere about this. . . . The purpose of tree protection ordinances is to protect trees and they should be made tight enough to do just that.'[1]

Today's guardians of New Zealand's notable trees follow a much broader path where the old-time Maori led with their dedication to the preservation of sacred trees. The pohutukawa was prominent among them.

Leadership in the mythological stakes obviously goes to the pohutukawa at Te Reinga whose blossoms are known as the flowers of spirits' flight, with a nod to Tangi te Korowhiti, the tree at Kawhia to which the Tainui canoe of the Great Fleet is said to have been moored. Sacred pohutukawa trees, while not abounding, are not too rare.

Such trees, either as single specimens or in coastal groves, identify perhaps the burial ground of a chief, an old battle site where warriors died, or even a tree which had cradled in death an honoured body, there to be swallowed while the tree grew round it and lived. Burial in this last-named manner meant the soul would be light and free forever compared with the depression and sadness which followed being covered with earth in burial. Pohutukawa planted to mark the birth of a chief's son were sacred.

In European times pohutukawa trees were a favoured choice in the upper half of the

North Island to commemorate special occasions, official and otherwise. Figures identi-fied with New Zealand history, including James Busby, Sir George Grey, Bishop Selwyn and Archdeacon L. W. Williams, planted pohutukawa trees which remain. There is the one in Customhouse Street, Gisborne, for instance, planted in 1892 to mark the opening of a new courthouse, or the pair in the small reserve near the Auckland Supreme Court which once flanked the main doorway of New Zealand's first Parliament House. Buildings decay and die; trees sometimes survive, and flourish.

Ensuring that trees prized for their historic, botanic or visual appeal are protected from wanton or accidental harm has been recognised as a matter of educating public awareness, a step towards which is the identification of such trees. As early as 1856 a paper on the cultivation and acclimatisation of exotic trees in New Zealand was prepared by Arthur Ludlam and subsequently published in the 1868 *Transactions and Proceedings of the New Zealand Institute*. Other contributions followed until a landmark catalogue of 153 historic trees was published in the *Journal of the New Zealand Institute of Horticulture*. Forty-eight of the trees were indigenous.

This list was compiled by Dr H. H. Allan after a New Zealand-wide tour and for long enough remained the published authority on the famous trees of New Zealand. Listing did not ensure protection, however, and age and the weather destroyed other trees.

The New Zealand Forest Service entered the recording scene in the 1960s with lists of historic and notable trees, including regional lists, but by far the most important catalogue of notable trees was compiled by a senior technical officer of the Forest Research Institute, S. W. (Bob) Burstall, who had joined that body in 1948 to work in the forest mensuration field.

Although Bob Burstall's assignment initially was to do with exotic forests, a keen personal interest extended his researches to non-forest trees and those of indigenous species. What began as a spare time hobby became an officially recognised project, to be pursued as and when other duties allowed. In the end he compiled 2668 individual descriptions as well as checklists of private aboreta. This material is unpublished.

Fortunately, a relatively short selection from Burstall's researches was culled by him and journalist E. V. Sale and published in 1984, in an attractive format, as *Great Trees of New Zealand*. The book included a main list of 100 trees plus a supplementary listing. The main list, say the authors, includes the trees 'which may be notable for their beauty as well as their size, for their occasional rarity as well as historical associa-tion'.[2] One baulks at the task they faced, of whittling a list of more than 2600 trees down to a selection of such modest dimensions. Where to end, what to discard, how to choose between exotic and indigenous trees, how to decide between historical and noteworthy size — all this and more must have taxed the authors' minds. They hint at the complexity of their task by noting that the selection is a personal one, 'not without the occasional compromise where a choice had to be made among specimens.'[3]

(Decay and storms helped reduce the choice. For instance, H. H. Allan's list of 153 historic trees was reduced to 15, as chosen by Burstall and Sale. And of these, only one was a pohutukawa, the famous tree at Te Araroa.)

In the culling process, the 24 entries of pohutukawa in Burstall's original list dwindled to nine in *Great Trees*, although under one of these entries there are sub-entries for another five. They range geographically from the famous pohutukawa at Te Reinga through Kawhia, Mangonui, Auckland, Te Araroa and the islands of Tiritiri Matangi, Kawau and Mayor, with a lone southern sentinel in Lower Hutt. Some are of venerable age, others deep-seated in Maori history, some sacred (and therefore not to be measured), some of European concern.

Wherever history has been made in New Zealand, there are trees, and in the northern half of the North Island, many of these historic trees are pohutukawa, each with its own story. Let us look at some.

Mayor Island

Off the East Coast of the North Island is bush-covered volcanic Mayor Island, today a base for big game fishing.

In 1916, when Lorna Cato was a member of a Napier group of 20 holidaying on the island, she and others of the party were enjoined not to walk in the shadow of a particular pohutukawa, a sacred tree. They respected the injunction, even if it was sometimes necessary to paddle the water's edge to avoid the shadow cast by the tree.

The group, whose journey from Napier in the vessel *Nga-apapa* took one and a half days, was landed by dinghy seven at a time. They met the island's residents — two Maori men in their seventies and one Maori woman in her eighties, bearing a moko. They did not have much English but on a first meeting with the old woman Lorna Cato was told of the tree, which was at the end of the beach on which they landed.

The name of the tree is Nga-uriapo (descendants of the past). Once partly destroyed by fire, Nga-uriapo has watched the passage of history, including a minor battle when other Maori came to the island. There are legends also of the tree's association with other dead.

Now a smoke-house operates under the spreading canopy of the tree; indeed, in its shadow.

Rotoiti

Inland and south of Mayor Island is Rotoiti, one of a pattern of lakes distinguished by sailing and fishing appeal. But Rotoiti has a pohutukawa appeal also.

The presence of pohutukawa on the lake's edges surprised a very early visitor, the German naturalist Ernst Dieffenbach, because they were trees he had never before found except on the seashore. 'This,' he concluded, 'may perhaps be regarded as another confirmation of the theory that the lakes which run in a continued chain from Taupo to the eastern coast are the remains of a former arm of the sea and have been shut up from each other by the uplifting of the land.'[4] (As mentioned earlier, many pohutukawa trees also grew round Lake Tarawera but were destroyed in 1886.)

Alternative suggestions as to the origin of the pohutukawa tree in this lakes region include seeding by birds and planting by wandering Maori, though some opinion holds that the very presence of the trees discounts both suggestions. Was Dieffenbach correct, therefore?

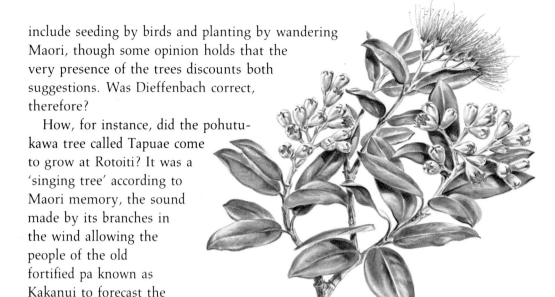

How, for instance, did the pohutukawa tree called Tapuae come to grow at Rotoiti? It was a 'singing tree' according to Maori memory, the sound made by its branches in the wind allowing the people of the old fortified pa known as Kakanui to forecast the weather.

'If its branches send a gentle "Mu-mu, mu, mu-mu," like the murmuring of a ngaro or [blow]fly, everything was calm and the lake would be smooth for canoeing and fishing,' Sir Maui Pomare and author James Cowan agreed in their *Legends of the Maori*. 'If it began to make a whistling sound, even though the wind was not high, it was a sign of an approaching marangai, a strong wind from the north-east, usually with rain; and if its cry rose to a shrill scream, its branches creaking and rubbing against each other, then presently a gale of wind would burst on the lake, and canoes had best keep to the beach.'[5]

Canoes have always been part of the Rotoiti scene since Maori occupation of the region, occasionally featuring in martial pursuits, and more than one such occasion involved the tree Tapuae.

Some 200 years ago the sister of the warrior chief Te Rangi-wawhia was insulted while living at the pa of Kakanui, at Ohoukaka, on Lake Rotoiti, where the pohutukawa Tapuae grew. Utu (revenge) had to be satisfied, so Te Rangi-wawhia mounted a war party of the Ngati Pikiao tribe against the Tuhourangi tribe and its well-sited and strongly fortified fort. But, being purportedly on friendly terms with the Tuhourangi, he split a small party from the main force and went to his sister's house, where they stayed.

The other warriors paddled silently up the lake that night and some hid among the shrubs and rocks at the foot of the steep cliff on which the Kakanui pa was perched. The rest waited till the dawn, then paddled their war canoes to the accompaniment of shouts of challenge and defiance. The defenders reacted promptly, launching their canoes and, with spear and war axe, fighting a small and lively naval battle.

Nor was Te Rangi-wawhia idle. In the darkness before dawn he tied a knotted flax rope to the base of the tree Tapuae, on the edge of the cliff, and threw the end to the warriors still silent in ambush below. When the war canoes were firmly engaged in

Wellington's Terrace pohutukawa was insured for $40,000 during nearby construction work, but provides priceless blessed relief in a concrete jungle.

battle, Te Rangi from next to the tree cried his whakaeraara-pa (a sentinel's watch-song) in challenge to his men below. It was time for them to join in the action:

Tika tonu mai,	Come straight this way,
Tika tonu mai,	To the spot where I now stand.
Kia ahau e noho nei	Straight towards me,
Tika tonu mai!	Straight this way, ha, ha![6]
I-a-ha-ha!	

His followers responded immediately, climbing the cliff face to join their chief under the tree Tapuae and from there engaged the warriors who had remained in the pa. With the advantage of complete surprise, they easily overwhelmed them. Meanwhile, Te Rangi's warriors were routing the Tuhourangi men on the water and soon the attack was complete — and successful.

Te Rangi's sister was taken to her former home up the lake. Te Rangi rested, his honour satisfied, his utu complete. And the pohutukawa called Tapuae lived on, a silent, scarlet memorial to this and many other incidents in the story of Lake Rotoiti.

Te Araroa

Age goes hand in hand with size in Te Waha-o-Rerekohu, the giant pohutukawa at Te Araroa, the township nearest East Cape whose name translates as the long pathway.

A canopy spread of almost 40 metres ensures a glorious sight when this magnificent pohutukawa is in bloom, while the tangle of branches (or trunks) from just above ground level confirms the age of the tree — at least 300 years. So it was a well-established tree when Captain James Cook sailed past in 1769. Today it is recognised as the oldest pohutukawa in the world.

The grass surrounding this massive tree is part of a reserve gifted by a direct descendant of the warrior for whom the tree is named. Rerekohu was a notable chief of the Te Araroa people some 260 years ago and the name given the tree is said originally to have been that of a large storehouse the chief had built and from which he generously distributed food to visitors. Hence the name translates as the mouth of Rerekohu.

Bob Burstall quoted another version, in which the construction of the storehouse is attributed to Rerekohu's father and the name given the building on the birth of Rerekohu, when tributes of food were brought for this male child of noble lineage and stored there. 'Both versions,' adds Burstall, 'agree that the Pohutukawa was growing near the storehouse and that Rerekohu transferred the name to it when he went to live at Hicks Bay and the storehouse fell into disuse.'[7]

The area is full of history. Three thousand people are said to have died or been captured under musket fire from an invading northern tribe in the 1820s.

In 1896, Professor H. B. Kirk of Victoria University College was writing in the *Transactions of the New Zealand Institute* of the road between Opotiki and Gisborne (which encompasses both Te Kaha and Te Araroa):

> From Te Kaha the track, where there is one, continues to skirt the coast. Here numbers and warlike habits of the old people are constantly recalled to mind by deep trench and bank cutting of all suitable points of land as fortifications. In many of the trenches pohutukawa a foot or more in diameter are now growing. . . .[8]

But if pohutukawa were — and are — a satisfying integral part of the scenic attractions of the East Coast, leaning protectively over almost every sandy beach and nodding a Christmas salute to passers-by, all pohutukawa roads on the coast lead back to the Te Araroa tree. It remains a distinctive botanical feature, a tree to be praised, to be talked about and admired. But its very existence was once endangered.

Retired Maori Affairs Department botanist, Harry Conway, of Gisborne, recalls measuring the Te Araroa pohutukawa almost 40 years ago for the Forest Service, when concern had been expressed about the tree blocking an entrance to the Te Araroa District High School. What could — and should — be done?

He advised that the tree should be left to continue to grow (as it is still doing), honouring the promise made by the government at the time the reserve was gifted to New Zealand that the tree would always be protected. A Forest Service report dated 3 October 1952 summarised the observations, over the signature of District Forest Officer A. M. Moore, who noted its enormous branch spread reached 37 metres at its widest point. He continued:

> The Te Araroa tree has 22 separate trunks which stem almost from ground level . . . The largest of the trunks is 43 inches in diameter and the smallest 13 inches. On the south and east sides the branches have an ascending habit whilst the north and west branches tend to be horizontal. . . . One dropping branch drags its twigs in the mud but I understand that it cannot be removed because of a clause in the original land-gift title which stated that the tree was not to be cut or interfered with in any way.
>
> The tree is certainly over 200 years old and possibly up to three times that age. The only method whereby the true age could be determined would be by taking an increment boring at ground level and thereby counting the annual rings. A ring-count of any of the individual trunks would not be a true indication of age as nobody could assess which was the first trunk to take form.
>
> According to local legend, the tree once stood on the water's edge but over the years the shore has been built up with debris washed down the Awatere River.

The Te Araroa pohutukawa possibly has a further claim to fame, in that it could be the tree called Oteko-mai-tawhiti which, according to Johannes Andersen, 'has this peculiarity that it is the first to bloom of all the pohutukawa on the coast'.[9] He did not identify the tree other than by its name, but the (then) Department of Lands and Survey, Gisborne, thought this was the tree to which he referred. Although, the department added, 'the statement that it is the first to flower should be viewed with caution.'[10]

Gisborne

Pohutukawa abound on the East Coast, but they are not taken for granted. For example, study the story of the impressive pohutukawa which guards the Gisborne Courthouse. But for public intervention, and a remarkable example of community co-operation, the tree would have been dumped after it was completely uprooted, according to former Gisborne MP Mrs Esme Tombleson, in an earthquake in the 1960s. The Ministry of Works saw no future for an unearthed tree, especially one of this size, but Esme Tombleson protested — by threatening to chain herself to the tree!

Not only was this pohutukawa a noble specimen but it claimed some historical authority in that the small tree from which it grew had been brought up the coast by horseback and planted on the site of the courthouse by a man called Barton, who became one of the first magistrates to serve Gisborne. The tree was shifted when a new courthouse was opened in 1962 to replace one burnt down.

Metrosideros tomentosa aurea, the yellow pohutukawa, found on Motiti Island about 1940.

Alerted by an officer of the Department of Labour in Gisborne that the MOW was planning to dump the uprooted tree, Mrs Tombleson 'intervened'. With the firm support of the Secretary for Justice, Dr John Robson, she enlisted community support to have the tree replanted. Nurseryman Bob Bayly of Wainui, who had just started his business, trimmed the tree's roots. The Fire Brigade undertook to keep the replanted tree watered. Contractors Monk Bros dug a hole and lent a crane to lift the tree back into position. Railways lent tarpaulins to cover the tree while it recovered. According to Mrs Tombleson, it would have cost more to dump the pohutukawa than it did to save it.

The tree did not fare well at first, in spite of the care given it, so Maori Affairs Department botanist Harry Conway was called in. He strengthened the base with new soil and put down a well, ostensibly to irrigate the courthouse garden, but the water went first to succour the pohutukawa. Moisture was essential to the recovery programme. He also lopped about two-thirds off the tree and sealed the cuts. The tree flourished thereafter.

While 'pruning' the tree — the operation was much more drastic, of course, but the

Te Waha-o-Rerekohu, the world's oldest and largest pohutukawa, is a much photographed
feature of the East Cape settlement of Te Araroa.

Community intervention and expert attention saved this magnificent pohutukawa in the
1960s. It guards the entrance to the Gisborne Courthouse.

effect was the same — Harry Conway was approached by a stranger who asked if he could take some of the larger limbs. He returned some time later with perfectly turned pohutukawa buttons, marketed, in sets of eight, on a small commercial scale as 'hand-made pohutukawa buttons'. On the reverse of the card of buttons was a description of *Metrosideros excelsa* and instructions on how to retain 'the full beauty of finish' while the garment on which they were used was washed, the whole printed under the injunction, 'Treasure these hand-made buttons from Gisborne NZ.'[11]

Harry Conway has another pohutukawa story to tell. Nature's exploitation of opportunity was demonstrated to him when he found a pohutukawa seedling about the size of a bedding plant in a crevice of the brick wall in the grounds of the government building at Gisborne. He gave the seedling an occasional watering and watched the plant send down a root to mother earth, in time strengthening to take over eventually as the main trunk. At the same time the plant continued to grow upwards until it became a full tree. 'This was an astonishing exhibition of survival by a young seedling Pohutukawa,' Mr Conway recalls. And he has a photograph to prove it.

Unfortunately, the MOW destroyed the tree during repair and maintenance work on the government buildings. What nature nurtures, man too often destroys.

Kawhia

Across the North Island, on the west coast, is Kawhia harbour, about halfway between New Plymouth and Auckland and the waterway entrance to the township of Kawhia, a nestling holiday resort. A pohutukawa tree on the beachfront has historic significance as the tree to which the crew of the Great Fleet canoe Tainui tied their craft when it was finally brought to rest.

Before that the Tainui canoe's cruise along the New Zealand coast had met with its fair share of incident. Landfall was in the Bay of Plenty where the crew found a whale fortuitously stranded on the beach, so the place was named Whangaparaoa (Sperm-whale Bay). The Tainui people tied a rope to the whale, ate some of its flesh and stripped its teeth for ornaments before venturing abroad to inspect this new country.

Then came the Arawa canoe, as eager as the Tainui to claim possession of the whale. They in turn tied a plaited rope to the carcase, and cunningly tied it to the whale, under the turns of the Tainui rope, scorching their own rope to age it. The ruse worked, the Tainui people being persuaded that their opponents had a prior claim because of the evident age of their rope. Tainui abandoned their stake and sailed away.

Nor was this the end of their misfortune. Sailing north under the command of the chief Hoturoa, the canoe beached briefly to allow a woman of rank, named Marama, to walk along the shore, accompanied by a slave attendant. They were recovered farther on. But when the crew tried to haul their canoe across the isthmus from the Tamaki arm of the Waitemata, the vessel could not be budged.

The truth must out. Marama saw her guilt reflected in the canoe's stubborn strength and, in Sir Peter Buck's words, 'revealed that she had demeaned herself with her slave'.[12] The canoe then slid forward and was portaged into the Manukau.

Members of the crew were dropped off along the west coast, the last party at Te Waiiti, where the canoe was left beached and unattended. When this became known, a party from Kawhia came overland and sailed the canoe back to Kawhia, where it was roped to the pohutukawa and where two stone uprights mark its length. The site is sacred. This tree is known as Tangi te Korowhiti but the long, low-lying branch to which the Tainui canoe was presumably moored was broken away.

From the earliest times, pohutukawa naturally decorated the seaside from about Gisborne across to Urenui north. Planting by the Maori and subsequently by Pakeha extended the spread of the trees to places south to Wellington, even to the South Island, some of the more notable trees becoming conspicuous.

The Burstall-Sale listings, for instance, include the noble pohutukawa at the Bellevue Hotel in Lower Hutt, a bequest from Arthur Ludlam who evidently planted the tree in the 1840s. A landmark pohutukawa greets shoppers at the Waikanae shopping centre, but pohutukawa are not hard to find in the Wellington area although they are introduced trees. Parliament's Beehive has its attendant pohutukawa grove, an appropriate legislative salute to a beautiful tree. Burstall also lists what he thinks was the first Anzac memorial in New Zealand, in the memorial tree at Eastbourne planted on Arbor Day 1915 (two and a half months after the landing at Gallipoli).

Add to these planned, commemorative plantings the random sowing of pohutukawa seed by horticultural enthusiasts. Muriel Fisher has recalled how, in the 1930s, the Wellington Beautifying Society planted pohutukawa on the bank of the Hutt Road and how, more recently, pohutukawa seed was sown on the clay banks of a newly widened Ngauranga Gorge in a bid to obliterate machine-made scars.[13]

Another horticultural enthusiast, Julian Matthews, has reported how the late James Stirling, for many years in charge of government gardens in Wellington, liked to scatter pohutukawa seed on bare ground such as new road cuttings, with the comment: 'Years from now people will wonder how pohutukawa come to be growing here.'[14]

There is no need to wonder how pohutukawa came to grow in the South Island, where it complements the high-flowering rata of the deeper forest. The pohutukawa has been introduced and is reported to be growing as far south as Stewart Island. The tree is an attractive novelty, so much so that a 7-metre tall specimen flowering in Christchurch in late January rated a five-column colour picture in the Christchurch *Press*. In the North Island such a picture would more likely have been printed in the immediate pre-Christmas period, not as a novelty but as a contribution to seasonal goodwill. Still it is pleasing to come across such trees south of Cook Strait, especially when in a grove, such as that in suburban Greymouth where 35-metre tall pohutukawa in Coronation Domain date from the 1920s, when a local doctor planted them.

Pohutukawa appear to best advantage in a seascape, their natural habitat, although they have the capacity to surprise by blooming in odd corners, in other people's gardens, as hedges and as boundary 'fences' in public reserves. Sometimes, however, they can be unwelcome. A pohutukawa tree in Napier, a big tree, which shades the sun from a living room in an overshadowed house, provided an opportunist platform for peeping-Toms who climbed up the tree to peek into upstairs bedroom windows. The Napier City Council decided that, while the tree undoubtedly had a nuisance value to the residents, its landscape appeal had to prevail and the tree remains one of five pohutukawa in the city protected under the district scheme.

Where pohutukawa grow into ripe old age, history merges with tradition to foster mythology and legend. These trees have become more than symbols; they include the sacred and the great.

At Kawhia harbour, the Tainui canoe of the Great Fleet was tied to a low pohutukawa branch. The tree remains but the branch has gone.

5
The New Beginnings

iven the right environment, pohutukawa live a very long time. The most famous specimen, the sprawling tree at Te Araroa, is reputed to be at least 300 years old, while pohutukawa centenarians are commonplace — that is, among those which survive. For, unfortunately, the pohutukawa is as susceptible as any other tree to the ravages of predators, opossums in particular. Their trail can be mapped all too easily in the Hauraki Gulf. The loss of trees is mourned but corrective action is being taken, in one instance by an inspired marshalling of voluntary labour.

This more recent devastation turns the clock back to the even more massive denudation of the whole Auckland scene as noted by shocked 19th-century visitors. While these time travellers could not have foreseen the damage wreaked by opossums (or cats, pigs, goats or rabbits), laid plain before them was the often wholesale destruction caused by Maori and Pakeha. What happened then cannot be repaired in the same way. In the 1850s Hochstetter looked at the 'now sterile soil [of a] sadly waste plain' where 'olden times luxuriant forest trees' once stood on the shores of the Waitemata harbour.[1]

When Hochstetter found something to admire, as with the Manukau harbour, he duly added his praise. His exploring party, for instance, landed in a small inlet for dinner 'under the shade of a magnificent pohutukawa tree, the trunk of which measured 24 feet in circumference'[2] against a background of rugged cliffs of a most remarkable appearance. The presence of the pohutukawa confirms that many of these trees escaped destruction because of their position on coastal cliffs quite unsuitable for cultivation.

But if Hochstetter regretted the absence of luxuriant forest which had been felled in the quest for cropping lands, he applauded the Auckland settlers — 'the town itself is in the country'[3] — for their 'beautiful gardens around the houses and where the clear sunny sky, not hidden by rows of four or five-storied houses, smiles upon every street where I say, on hearing somebody in Auckland speaking of longing after country life, we could hardly refrain from smiling at such an idea.' The inhabitants he found 'happy'.[4]

Naturalist Ernst Dieffenbach agreed with Hochstetter about the destruction of the forests, but took time out during an expedition on the Hauraki Gulf to note the presence of *Metrosideros tomentosa* among other trees on the cliff face. Also present were the puriri, the toru, rewarewa, the New Zealand tree fuchsias and the karaka as well as some of the lower shrubs. 'But this vegetation is merely confined to the coast as the land, which extends from the north shore of Manukau is not covered with anything of higher growth than fern, rushes. . . . The whole has formerly been covered with kauri-forest, as is proved by the gum or resin, of which pieces are everywhere found . . .'[5]

Not everyone saw the changing face of the land as something to be mourned. The 'Father of Auckland', John Logan Campbell, a successful councillor and mayor, could find much satisfaction in 'the glorious landscape . . . [where] open country stretched away in vast fields and fern, and Nature reigned supreme'. This fern, which had replaced the forests, was, in turn, succeeded by 'green fields which gladdened the eye; the white gleam of the farmer's homestead dots the landscape . . . White sails skim along the water, and the black smoke can be seen of many a steamer as it cuts its way, passenger-laden; and last, but not least, the loudest, with its screech of civilisation, the locomotive on the iron road proclaims, "I have reclaimed the wilderness and made the desert place glad".'[6]

This 1840 perspective was extended during an expedition on the Waitemata where Campbell noted 'the full rich carol of the tui or parson bird from the brushwood skirting the shore',[7] and a landing at a small shelly beach (Orakei) at the base of some lovely wooded slopes. No pohutukawa here — wrong time of year perhaps.

Man can do little to save flora from natural disasters but he can attempt rehabilitative measures in the wake of damage and loss caused by natural predators, although too often the corrective efforts are belated. Special attention is being given to the regeneration of pohutukawa in the Hauraki Gulf Maritime Park islands, but elsewhere there are voices crying in a pohutukawa wilderness, unheeded by authority because, a district conservator has alleged, a problem with local body pest control is that ratepayers prefer to see their rates spent on the protection of horticultural crops and farmlands.[8]

An Auckland University botanist, Dr Neil Mitchell, reported in 1987 that aerial photographs showed a 40 percent loss of pohutukawa through opossum damage in five years at the Mangonui Bluff reserve, with many trees also killed in the Bay of Islands and the Cape Rodney areas. Could the pohutukawa thus become an endangered species? He thought so.[9]

Wallabies as well as opossums wreaked havoc among the pohutukawa of Kawau Island, to the point where in 1985 it was forecast that if no major pest control work was carried out the 'pohutukawas will disappear from the island by 1990'.[10] It was estimated that 99 percent of the pohutukawa on the island's southern and eastern coastal slopes had been killed by defoliation and at least 30 percent on the northern and western shores, with the remaining trees at risk from heavy browsing.

Only a few pohutukawa now grow in the valley behind Bosanquet Bay on the southern coast of Kawau Island and a couple of pockets of beech trees, while the trees of the 'banqueting hall' area are now puriri and taraire. The banqueting hall was notorious as the setting for a cannibal feast — with bleached bones as convincing evidence — held probably towards the end of the 18th century when mainland tribes united in an expedition to eradicate marauding Ngatitai who used Kawau as a base from which to launch piratical attacks on canoes passing up the gulf.

Rehabilitation and conservation measures are restoring growth on Kawau Island, with wallaby and opossum numbers under the strict control of a full-time animal control officer.

Even more satisfying is the regeneration programme on Tiritiri Matangi (where the wind blows) Island, part of the Hauraki Gulf Maritime Park since 1976. Pakeha farming meant that the last stands of bush were confined to steep-sided ravines, while predatory creatures abounded. A successful elimination programme has cleared the way for an ambitious replanting programme, initially with pohutukawa, as part of an Open Sanctuary project. Rare and endangered forest species are being introduced and bird life encouraged, such as native parakeets and bellbirds which are no longer seen in or near Auckland city. Public access is free during daylight, but camping is prohibited in an attempt to keep the island free from rats, which have a habit of escaping from boats at night.

Financial support from the World Wildlife Fund and other organisations has enabled the nursery on Tiritiri, run by lighthouse keeper Ray Walter, to produce 30,000 trees and shrubs a year, from seed gathered from trees on the island. (Pohutukawa seeds are not hard to find, the average number of seeds in each capsule being about 850, according to Auckland botanist Dr Laurie Millener. He estimated that one particular tree on Rangitoto Island in the superb 'pohutukawa summer' of 1946–47 produced some 40 million seeds.)

Planting the seedlings has been a community chore carried out by volunteers from Auckland — bring your lunch, a spade and $10 for the launch fare! And they have responded, people of all ages and from all walks of life, as the *Sunday Star* put it: 'practising or retired knobbly-kneed scientists, doctors, farmers, accountants, bank managers, scholars, solicitors, artists, Boy Scouts, even literary critics and ordinary happy-looking hoi-polloi nature-lovers, their wives and progeny.' Such co-operative effort gives meaning to conservation, while the choice of pohutukawa for the initial plantings — some thousands of them — should restore a natural pohutukawa paradise.

Indeed, Tiritiri Matangi boasts a very old pohutukawa, above a valley from a beach on the south side of the island, with the exceptional spread of 32 metres, as recorded by Burstall and Sale. This tree was thus once acclaimed as having the largest span of any pohutukawa anywhere, but a branch was lost during a severe storm in 1986.

Tiritiri Matangi, as the largest of the Hauraki Gulf islands, is an appropriate choice for an ambitious regeneration project, but other islands host their pohutukawa, some of venerable age, along with old stories of life and death. There is Little Barrier Island (Hauturu), New Zealand's first government nature reserve, where a tangled pohutu-kawa grove invites visitors to tread softly amid the interlaced trunks and aerial roots. This grove, known as Pua Mataahu, is sacred as the burial ground of warriors who

The aerial roots which descend from a mature pohutukawa perform a
breathing function and anchor the tree.

Artist unknown. *Doorway of St. Stephen's chapel, Taurarua.* [1863?]
Watercolour with egg tempera, 16·1 × 18·8 cm. *Alexander Turnbull Library*

disputed possession of the island, possibly in the mid-17th century. Hauturu (the wind's resting-post) is supposed to be the centrepost of the great net of Taeamainuku, which he cast across the Hauraki Gulf from Cape Colville to the Whangarei Heads. The Hen and Chicken Islands were reputedly the corks.)

Farther south, opposite Rangitoto Island, is onshore Takapuna where, between the beach and the Mon Desir Hotel, stands the largest pohutukawa on the mainland of the greater Auckland area. Its spreading branches identify the start of a sacred grove of pohutukawa, known as Te Urutapu, extending about a kilometre to Thorne Bay. Wayfarers paid tribute by hanging an article of clothing on the trees or placing a sprig of fern or manuka at their feet.

In summer dress these pohutukawa make a brilliant display along the near shore-line. Small surprise, therefore, that the Takapuna City Council in 1987 resolved to call their area the Pohutukawa Coast, complementing the Hibiscus Coast immediately to the north. A council committee on tourism, along with the Takapuna Business Associ-ation and the North Shore Local Bodies Association, is promoting the name.

Auckland city's schedule of trees compiled under its district scheme lists 114 trees, from oaks and eucalyptus to totara and kauri. Twelve of the listings are pohutukawa, most being included for their visual amenity classification.

Of those classified as historic, the sprawling giant alongside St Stephen's Chapel in Parnell is a magnificent and living tribute to Bishop Selwyn, the missionary bishop whose 26 years' service in New Zealand saw the establishment of the Anglican Church as the pre-eminent Christian institution in New Zealand. Selwyn, known to scatter acorns during his strolls, is considered almost certain to have planted this Parnell pohutukawa under which tombstones now shelter, bearing dates from the 1850s on.

A bird's eye view would locate another magnificent pohutukawa in the Parnell Rose Gardens, claimed by Burstall and Sale as 'the largest and best-sited pohutukawa to have been planted by a European'.[11] It is thought to have been planted about 1850 and is certainly worth a Christmas visit.

But not all pohutukawa trees come to life from planted seedlings. The situation of the pohutukawa seed which found a niche in a Gisborne wall has been repeated time and time again. Another seed won recognition in a 1973 *New Zealand Herald* editorial, a Saturday contribution which bears all the hallmarks of 'Grammaticus' (the much-loved Professor E. M. Blaiklock). 'A small Easter parable', he called the pohutukawa seed which had lodged in the massive bole of two black and rugged trunks of an ancient pine which, in its youth, looked over the wall of Albert Barracks in what is now Albert Park near the Auckland City Art Gallery.

Said the *Herald* editorial: 'If ever the old sentinel pine dies at its barracks post, it is to be hoped that the woodmen will contrive to leave the great stump so that its death may feed new vigour, and centuries of life, to a native tree, whose crimson bloom inspired the late Father Forsman's Christian hymn. It is a symbol which surely must be kept.' The editorial then dwelt on the familiar Easter message — 'From death comes life . . .'.[12]

The pohutukawa survives although, according to Roger Blackley, curator of historical New Zealand art at the Auckland City Art Gallery, it 'is probably destined to remain a bonsai for as long as the pine tree stands'.[13]

Auckland, while certainly important, is but one centre of the pohutukawa landscape. The tree grows naturally there, it claims historic roots and it gives the Christmas season a sense of colourful warmth, but the city does not stand above others. Move up the newly dubbed Pohutukawa Coast and enjoy its Christmas season. Or to places farther north, such as the entrance to Mangonui harbour, and other Burstall and Sale identifications — Assassination Cove in Manawaroa Bay, halfway between Russell and Cape Brett in the Bay of Islands, where the French explorer Marion du Fresne is said to have been killed under the pohutukawa there on 12 June 1772; or the tree at the southeast corner of the Treaty House verandah at Waitangi, reputed to have been planted by James Busby about 1860; and in Taranui Bay, Bay of Islands, where one of the Great Fleet canoes is said to have landed and the tree was used by Maori to hang the heads of their human victims.

It is no responsibility of this text to seek to identify all the more famous of the pohutukawa trees of New Zealand — the historic or the botanically attractive. Burstall and Sale have done that. Moreover, district schemes are now listing these precious trees which, in turn, are guarded by the voluntary members of tree societies and other such groups, to our good fortune and posterity's benefit.

Few would deliberately seek pohutukawa landscapes — they are more something to savour along the way, to treasure in memory — but to find a pohutukawa Christmas parade, where should one turn? Various partisan public relations officers would provide an answer, many with some authority.

The Wenderholm recreation area north of Waiwera has been nominated as a very special pohutukawa reserve because of the grove planted by Maori prisoners of war. Go to Auckland, obviously, and north up the coast where the pohutukawa waves crimson banners in seasonal greeting. And down the East Coast, to celebrate the season with neighbours of the Te Araroa sovereign.

Or take a sidepath, to the Coromandel Peninsula. According to recorded legend, there are no especially historic trees, though there must be some hidden among the groves which crowd the coastline. Maurice Shadbolt has described the physical details of the peninsula and its pohutukawa inhabitants in the giant groves between Colville and Port Jackson, adorning 'the magnificent seascapes and lonely corners' of Coromandel. In other days, when camping was permitted on the coast here, campers picnicked among the pohutukawa groves, enjoying the freedom of space, air and beauty.

Wherever in New Zealand you may be, pause when you see a magnificent pohutukawa in seasonal finery, admire it, praise it, ask about its history. Perhaps it has a story all its own; perhaps a Selwyn or a Busby or some other amateur botanist ventured to plant pohutukawa because of a hunger in his heart for something akin to the Christmas holly of the old world.

6
The Flowers
of Spirits' Flight

y far the most famous tree in Maori mythology is the pohutukawa which guards the entrance to the sacred cave at Cape Reinga through which the disembodied spirits of the dead pass to their resting place in the next world. Some opinion holds that the next world in this context is within the far regions of the west, the original fatherland of the New Zealand Maori, along the Ara Whanui a Tane (the broad path of Tane), which is the golden path of the Pacific. The westernmost capes are the leaping-off places of the spirits, their last association with the land of the living as, for the final time, they follow the trail of the setting sun.

'Far away shalt thou fly, to the north land's end,' sings the traditional Maori lament:

Ki ro kauwhau o te riri,	Far away shalt thou fly, to the
Ka rere koe	north land's end
I te Hiku o te Ika e-e!	(The land of spirits' flight — the
	land of death).[1]

So to Cape Reinga the spirits travel, to this surf-washed promontory where, as James Baxter noted in 1961, a lighthouse guides the living to a haven for the dead.[2]

The cape is at the tip of New Zealand, bordered on the west by the neighbouring promontory of Cape Maria van Diemen and, to the east, by North Cape. Spirits Bay, which curves to the east from Cape Reinga, is where the kuaka (godwits) gather for their annual flight to breeding grounds in north-eastern Siberia and north-western America.

Spirits Bay is not named, as one might assume, for some rollicking days of old with the demon rum. Rather, the name comes from Maori belief associated with Cape Reinga itself. For when Maori heard the rustle of the wings of some belated bird passing overhead towards the cape, they mourned another spirit passing to its rest. If the rustling noise continued, on and on, it was but sorry confirmation that a mighty battle had been fought — with great losses. This they knew long before the intelli-

The most famous pohutukawa in Maori mythology, the tree at Te Reinga, from which the
spirits of the dead descend to the underworld.

gence arrived by more usual means. And even in such death there was class distinction, for the souls of slaves were channelled beneath the raised food stores (pataka) while those of the chiefs passed to one side.

Farther east again is Tom Bowling Bay, into which runs the stream Kapo-Wairua, which means snatching souls, a reference to the evil attempts of the demons which snatch at the spirits of the dead as they journey to Muriwhenua, their leaping-off place at land's end.

The journey is never comfortable, for there is so much to forget as the spirits travel just inland of Ninety Mile Beach. So they stop to look back and weep in high, wailing voices, like the whistling wind; they lacerate themselves with flakes of obsidian, as was the practice at funeral gatherings. Greenery, not always common in the district, is woven into death chaplets for their heads, while their trail is marked by knotted sandhill grasses, a memento of their passing.

Sir Maui Pomare recorded that the green leaves and twisted grasses left by the spirits as tokens of their passage varied according to whether the spirit came from the interior (small bundles of leaves of the nikau palm) or the coast (a seaside grass, the pingao). Knots are also tied in the wind-tattered blades of flax growing on the stony ridges and sand dunes. 'These flax leaves, say some, are twisted together by the gales that sweep across Muriwhenua's wastes. Bu the Maori knows they are the signs left by the vanished ones, tied by the spirits to show who comes after them the way they have gone to the land of night.'[3]

What greenery there was along death's passage to the farewell pohutukawa at Cape Reinga was removed over the years. Ernst Dieffenbach was moved to comment that 'Where the kauri once grew the soil is now only fit for the manuka and the fern. Evidence that this over-whelming sand drift is of modern date, and is owing to the destruction of the forest, may be seen on the western coast'.[4] What man once destroyed, man today is seeking to repair, through the northern afforestation programmes, notably among the sand dunes lapping the coast.

And so along the knife-back ridge and up the hill to look down upon the leaping place at Te Reinga and the great tree of Maori mythology which, according to some tradition, is 1200 years old. The branches which lent down to the surf, a bridgeway from life to the portals of the dead, have been broken off. Some question whether this is in fact the original tree; is it, rather, a truncated version of a tree which has survived the centuries? But a pohutukawa it most certainly is, whose blossoms are known in legend as Te Pua o te Reinga — the flowers of spirits' flight:

> Grim, gaunt and weird,
> Adorned with strange fantastic arms
> It stands: a silent beacon
> To departing shades;
> A leafy portal to the gates
> Of dark and mystic worlds.[5]

Beneath the Te Reinga pohutukawa was the gateway of the hereafter, Tatau-o-te-Po, a swirling tideway guarded by the seaweed to which the roots and the branches of the tree reached down. According to Sir Maui Pomare, it was here that, 'with the seafowl screaming their requiem, the winds of Land's End whistling about the cape, the ocean murmuring in a thousand voices, the Wairua Maori departed from this land of Aotearoa'.[6] Always there was the dream of what Pomare called 'the mystic profundity', through the ocean door of Po, on the trail of the setting sun.

One account puts an extra obstacle at the very entrance to the Reinga underworld, a stream called Waiora-a-Tane, where a last vetting for admission to the hereafter took place. Some travelling spirits, indeed, were allegedly refused admission and required to return, under the strictest conditions, to their human bodies to resume their lives. The concept of a final stream bridging the worlds of life and death echoes other older places. The immediate comparison is with the river Styx and its guardian ferryman Charon. A water barrier would make sense to the islanders of the south-west Pacific, especially as they looked north over the ocean to their legendary homeland of Hawaiki. For that matter, every primitive race associated death with the setting of the sun; from New Zealand, the aspect was north-west. Hence the lament, 'Wait, wait awhile, O sun, and we'll go down together.'[7] The sinking sun and the sinking soul, both moving westward into darkness, may rise together.

Pioneer missionary Samuel Marsden knew of the Te Reinga doctrine. In 1820, while at Kaipara, he wrote: 'They said that all the souls of the New Zealanders went when they died to a cave at North Cape and from thence descended into the sea to the next world.'[8] Not all European recorders of the tradition were enamoured of the belief; Marsden certainly was not. What he referred to as 'the bondage of superstition' provoked a desire among some critics to demolish the Maori creed in favour of European Christianity. Fortunately, both critics and observers patiently recorded the story of Te Reinga and its guardian pohutukawa, so that the whole tradition has been handed down remarkably, if not wholly, complete.

Te Reinga's significance has been well documented from the earliest European times. The earliest recorded evidence dates back to 1793, when the tohunga Tuki Tahua from the Doubtless Bay area drew a map of the Reinga apex, including the pohutukawa tree, for the benefit of Governor King of Norfolk Island.

The tree appears to be of somewhat straggly growth, though of a good size with what could possibly be four main branches. One 'branch', pointing east-north-east before bending sharply southwards towards the land, may be intended to represent the main root down which the souls plunged to the kelp-ridden pool which was the door to the underworld and was owned by the female guardian of the underworld, Hine-nui-te-Po. (According to that inspired public servant and keen amateur ethnologist Edward Tregear, the proverbial Maori saying that 'He has slid down the pohutukawa tree' meant 'He is dead'.)[9]

A double line on the sketch, traced by Governor King's secretary at Tuki Tahua's bidding, swings down the western coast of Ea-hei-no-maue, Tuki's name for the North

Island, and is noted as 'the road which goes the length of Ea-hei-no-maue', presumably the route travelled by the spirits to Te Reinga. It is particularly interesting that the secretary, again presumably on Tuki Tahua's identification, wrote 'Terry-inga' beside the picture of the tree. There have, no doubt, been worse phonetic interpretations of Te Reinga's spelling.

Most Te Reinga accounts dwell primarily on the washing waves beneath the pohutukawa and the rocks against which the water 'beat for ever from below the sound of wailing and lamentation. The waters rushed upwards, the beds of floating kelp were swirled aside and the path stood revealed. Here was Haumu, the entrance to the Shades'.[10]

This nether world was a twilight place, where progress could be discerned. And there was a wall to pass, said some. If the soul passed above the wall which barred the way, it could yet return to earth, but if it went underneath the wall it had to abandon hope.

Having passed beneath the wall, therefore, the soul came to a lake surrounded by hills — and the shades of the dead waiting on the banks. The newcomer looked to find departed friends or relations, preferably someone from the same family. But even these could prove false friends, offering welcome and food. If accepted, such food would ensure that the partaker dwelt thenceforth in 'The Land of No Return'.

Thousands of godwits gather at Cape Reinga and Spirits Bay for their long flight north to breeding grounds in Siberia and north-western America.

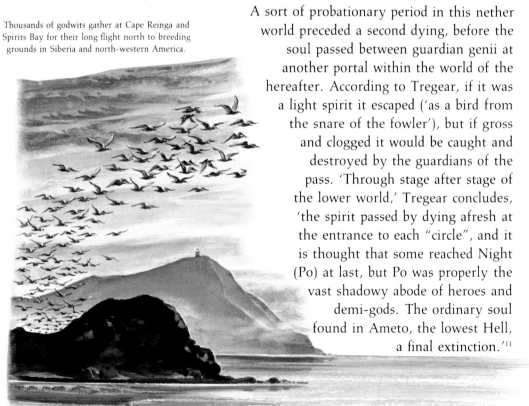

A sort of probationary period in this nether world preceded a second dying, before the soul passed between guardian genii at another portal within the world of the hereafter. According to Tregear, if it was a light spirit it escaped ('as a bird from the snare of the fowler'), but if gross and clogged it would be caught and destroyed by the guardians of the pass. 'Through stage after stage of the lower world,' Tregear concludes, 'the spirit passed by dying afresh at the entrance to each "circle", and it is thought that some reached Night (Po) at last, but Po was properly the vast shadowy abode of heroes and demi-gods. The ordinary soul found in Ameto, the lowest Hell, a final extinction.'[11]

But it was not inevitably final, again according to Tregear, for some souls were said to return to earth as flies and some as moths,[12] a more attractive end, perhaps, than that quoted by another 19th-century student of the Maori, T. W. Gudgeon, who tells of man passing through various divisions in the internal structure of Te Reinga until he comes to a final apartment, Toke, where the soul becomes a worm, 'which worm returns to the earth and when a worm dies, man's being is ended.'[13]

In the end, of course, all souls met the shades of Reinga and disappeared into the land of the hereafter; there could be no escaping fate. But sometimes, it seems beyond doubt, the end could be postponed!

Sir Maui Pomare acknowledged having 'heard many a story of imaginary visits to the Reinga and of the return to this land of light, the Ao-Marama'.[14] He could quote the story of a Wairoa woman who, to all appearances dead, revived and lived for some days. She was able to give a vivid description of her visit to the underworld where she met the souls of people she had known in their life.

Historian John White (1821–91), in his time the outstanding Pakeha authority on Maori language and culture, told of two venturesome women who went 'to the point on which grows the pohutukawa tree, down the roots of which the spirits descend. They descended . . . and, after adjusting their hair and garments, they entered the mouth of the cave'.[15]

John White's raconteur was the wife of a tribal chief, Te Rou, described in his tale simply as 'Te Rou's wife'. A spirited woman, at a marae war council she responded on behalf of her sex when taunted by another chief:

> If women could do in battle as much as they can with their tongues, men would cook and do their work. If women were what they should be, their love would make men brave. What do you know of war? . . . You boast that you are nearer to the gods than we are. Shall I refresh your childish memories of the truth that two women, braver than men ever were, once went into the world of spirits alive? You cannot now remember it, and as I know something of teaching children, I will teach you.

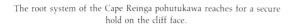

The root system of the Cape Reinga pohutukawa reaches for a secure hold on the cliff face.

The story she had to tell was of two courageous women, who wished to know what sort of a place Reinga really was, 'not altogether believing the tales invented by foolish men about the abode of spirits.' Each with a kit of sweet potato (kumara) on her back, the two women

> went to the point on which grows the pohutukawa tree, down the roots of which the spirits descend [and] . . . entered the mouth of the cave. . . . They journeyed until the light of this world no longer enlightened the cave; they had gone such a distance!
> They went on in the dark, and at last saw, at a great distance, a small, bright speck which, on approaching, they discovered to be a fire, by which sat three grey-headed, white-bearded skeleton spirits, warming themselves. The fire was made of three sticks only. You all know that the fire of a sick man is sacred; also that of a priest; how much more so the fire of spirits?[16]

One of the women said, 'We must have some of that fire.' The other agreed and at last one went and took a firestick.

According to Te Rou's wife, the three old priests were so astonished on seeing the intruders, that they sat still for some time, no doubt afraid. The women threw down their baskets of kumara, 'thus doing an act of kindness, giving the spirits some of the food they liked while in this world.' Then the women started for the world of the living as fast as they could, the one with the firestick being behind.

Te Rou's wife continued:

> The first had got back to this world, outside the mouth of the cave; and just as the other, with the fire, was in the act of taking the last step out, one of the old spirits . . . caught her by the heels. She knew if he got the firestick no one would be able to know what fire they had in Reinga, so with all her strength threw the firebrand away from her into the air as far as she could; her strength was so great that it went up and stuck in the clouds. Do you see the moon? Then thank a woman for the light it gives. That is the firebrand.

Te Rou's wife was not finished: 'Could man have outrun a spirit? Could man have thrown it to the sky? . . . Yes, you have not seen the gods, and women have, and have been in the abode of the gods. . . . Go learn of women sense and wisdom.'[17]

Such is one version of the origin of the moon, rescued from a hiding place beneath the Te Reinga pohutukawa.

A much more recent subterranean adventurer was Ngakahikatea, who lived with her granddaughter in the Mangatea Valley east of Ohinewai. She died in 1975 when, according to author Michael King in his *Being Pakeha*, a thick fog rolled off the Waikato River and covered the district for four days. Her family laid her body out on the marae in preparation for the tangi, while her spirit travelled northwards to the 'Leaping-off Place of Spirits' where, after cleansing herself, she stood on the ledge from which hung Te Aka, the pohutukawa root. Below was Maurianuku, the entrance to the underworld, covered by a curtain of seaweed.

As she prepared to grasp the root and slide down to the entrance, she was challenged: 'Who is it?' 'I have come to be with my parents,' she replied. Then came the ruling: 'They do not want you yet. Eat nothing and go back where you came from until they are ready.'

So she rose, returned to her body and her people: 'My family and those who had assembled from Waihi for the tangi were most surprised when I breathed again and sat up. So it is,' she told Michael King, 'that I live on.'[18]

Dr Edward Shortland (1812–93), Maori linguist and student of Maori lore, also had a back-from-the-dead tale. His servant's aunt, a woman of rank, died and the body was sealed in her hut on the banks of Lake Rotorua. Her spirit departed for Te Reinga, to encounter near her destination an outsize bird (taller than a man) which frightened her into a canoe, in which she was ferried across a river (the river of the dead). In a village on the far bank she met her father and many near relatives, all of them dead, who welcomed her and began a tangi (the wailing extempory chant addressed to people met after a long absence).

Afterwards her father questioned her about his living relatives, particularly about her child. 'Then,' he said, 'you must go back to earth, for there is no one left to take care of my grandchild. But remember, if you once eat food in this place you never more return to life; so beware not to taste anything offered you.'[19]

She resisted the temptation of a basket of baked kumara and succeeded in returning to her own house, after luring off two infant spirits whose efforts to detain her were thwarted when she threw them two huge kumara. She was welcomed back, her tale was believed, but there was general regret that she had not brought back at least one of the giant kumara.

Most souls, however, were given their sanctuary in the world beyond Te Reinga, beneath the pohutukawa blossom known as the flowers of spirits' flight. As an ancient song of the Maori begins:

E tomo e Pa,	Enter, O Sire,
Ki Murimuri-te-Po,	The Gates of that Dark Land
Te Tatau-o-te-Po . . .	The Door of the Endless Night . . .[20]

The Te Reinga beliefs are part of Maori tradition. Christian missionaries offered an alternative version of what happened after death and the Maori in time came mostly to accept this teaching. But when the winds rustle along the pathway to the cape, what messages do they whisper? Is their content changed?

7
A War-time Salute

rom a 2nd NZEF battleground in the Middle East of World War II came *A Pohutukawa Carol*, a home-thoughts-from-abroad salute to the Christmas tree of far-off New Zealand to which Kiwi servicemen, wherever they were stationed, inevitably turned their thoughts at that season.

The words of the carol and the music to accompany them were written by Father E. A. (Ted) Forsman, a chaplain serving with the New Zealanders before and during the Sidi Rezegh action in the Libyan Desert in November–December 1941.

The New Zealand Division suffered considerable casualties in killed, wounded and prisoners taken at the hands of the Afrika Korps before a relief column punched its way through to Tobruk to lift the long German siege of Australian soldiers trapped in that city and port.

Father Forsman was taken prisoner during this campaign when the Afrika Corps overran a New Zealand advanced dressing station and, fluent in German and Italian, he conversed with General Rommel's aide-de-camp. It so happened that at the time of the latter's arrival New Zealand doctors were trying to save the shattered arm of a German soldier, a fact which helped to ensure a favourable response when Father Forsman sought replenishment of their meagre water supply — a full tanker duly arrived in a very short time. After about a week a South African Division recaptured the compound.

How, then, did Father Forsman come to write this Christmas carol with the backdrop of war, amid the hideous noise, the dust, the acute suffering of the badly wounded and the sudden death?

The answer begins with Father Forsman's great-grandfather, Sergeant-major Patrick Fitzpatrick, and his family landing from the *Minerva*, one of the first groups of sailing ships, at Howick Beach in 1847. The Fitzpatricks were granted a small parcel of land beneath Pigeon Mountain in Pakuranga and down the generations the family lived close to the Pakuranga area, bounded to the west by the Tamaki River. Barn Beach (now Half Moon Bay) was a semi-private retreat used on legion occasions each year by

The coastline on the Coromandel Peninsula is famous for the abundance of pohutukawa trees.

A Pohutukawa Carol

E.A. Forsman. Arr. Moor-Karoly.

the whole Forsman family. Leading down to Barn Beach, and indeed all around the adjacent coastline, were large stands of pohutukawa trees.

Small wonder, then, that, while ministering to soldiers thousands of kilometres from home, locked in a fierce and bloody battle for freedom, Father Ted, with Christmas approaching, should have in his mind's eye the Barn Beach blaze of colour. He returned to New Zealand with the first leave draft of the home furlough scheme and it was then his longstanding musician friend Professor Moor-Karoly agreed with pleasure to write the original musical accompaniment to *A Pohutukawa Carol*, an arrangement from a musical theme developed by the father, who was steeped in the polyphonic music and plain chant glories of his era. Thus was he able to bring to his *Pohutukawa Carol* an intertwining of music and words reminiscent of compositions from the golden centuries of liturgical music. It was Professor Moor-Karoly's arrangement which Father Forsman used on his Christmas card.

Now crimson, crimson Christmas trees
　　Pohutukawas rim our seas
And flower in flame on every shore
　　For joy of him whom Mary bore.

Chorus: Babe so poor and small,
　　Jesus God of all,
　　O with us abide,
　　This Holy Christmas-tide.

Such trees gave wood to make His cot,
　　And all His toys from trees he got,
And when he came to ply a trade
　　He shaped from trees the things he made.

Because a tree had brought us doom,
　　Was Jesus born of Mary's womb,
To blossom high on Calvary's tree,
　　The crimson bloom that makes us free.

Long raise, O trees, about our land,
　　Your crimson sign on every strand
That we may tell each Christmas morn
　　Why Jesus was of Mary born.

As one of his former parishioners recalls, Father Forsman 'greatly loved his country and never forgot the war years.

'He was from a very musical family . . . and he had a resonant voice and a knowledge of music. He was quite a personality, deeply religious, a part-time lecturer at our university [Auckland] and a great follower of cricket and always a simple parish priest, loved by his parishioners.'

Upon the expiration of his allocated home furlough, Father Forsman returned to the 2nd NZEF in the Middle East and served out the war. He died in Auckland in August 1976. May he rest in peace.

8
Pohutukawa and Poets

his was the title that classical scholar Professor E. M. Blaiklock gave to Chapter Six of his book *Green Shade*, in which he wrote of the pohutukawa ('in many ways the most regal of New Zealand trees'), and of Pindar, Father Forsman, Alfred Domett, Tennyson and Browning, a full measure of poets to complement this special tree. And he wished for more, in that, 'with passing time perhaps, and the emergence of our poets from their urban preoccupations, someone will find the poetry of native trees'.[1]

Father Forsman, he thought, was moving in the right direction with his *Pohutukawa Carol*, 'when it caught the thought of the blood-red bloom, bursting luxuriantly forth at Christmas-time, in tribute . . . to the Calvary that followed Bethlehem':

> Now crimson, crimson Christmas trees,
>   And flowering flame on every shore,
> Pohutukawa rim our seas
>   For joy of Him whom Mary bore.[2]

Not every New Zealand poet was quoted with approval by this talented and discerning scholar.

But before this contribution to pohutukawa poetry came that abortive epic, Alfred Domett's *Ranolf and Amohia*, noted by the professor for its botanical accuracy. The poem's other claim to more than passing attention is that it was written by a man who was Prime Minister of New Zealand from August 1862 to October 1863 and who was also an efficient administrator in land matters. His lifelong interest in literature was reflected in his verse (including translations of Maori myths), his naming of the streets of Napier after English poets and essayists (while he was Commissioner of Crown Lands in Hawke's Bay) and his friendship with Robert Browning. His verse was anthologised by Longfellow.

The Cascade falls at Karekare on the west coast, near Auckland.

Full credit to Domett, in any case, for his description of the usual seaside habitat of the pohutukawa:

> The stony faces of the cliffs thus rent
> Showed twisted strata strangely earthquake bent.
> From crest and crevice, tortuously flung,
> Those monstrous iron-hearted myrtles hung,
> Stiff, snaky, writhing trunks, and roots that clave
> And crawled to any hold the ramparts gave.[3]

Whoever has paused to consider the tenuous hold of the tree on a cliffside, with the aerial roots dropping down, will respect Domett's study.

Among the more recent New Zealand poets who have found time and words to honour the pohutukawa, the Christian ethic is a familiar theme. Almost all link the tree with Christmas; to them the 'Christmas tree' is just that. Fay Clayton, however, uses the image of the Cross of Calvary in her poem, *Pohutukawa*:

> Your twisted trunk stands
>   naked to the wind and sun,
> And His scourged body too
>   knew shameful elevation.
> Your tortured branches
>   and His outstretched arms,
> Speak agony of hours.
>
> Your roots hump out
>   as did His feet
> In sudden awkward spasm;
>   and for you both
> Pohutukawa and the Man,
>   your final glory
> Lies in scarlet flowers.[4]

Cynthia Watson, in *Some Flora of Aotearoa*, lists clematis, kowhai and manuka before acknowledging:

> then comes our Christmas Tree?
> Pohutukawa, red!
> Enflaming hearts and coasts
> (O remember what the angel said?)
> Then drop your crimson carpet for Emanuel,
> God and the Virgin's child . . .[5]

Others write from a Polynesian base. Hone Tuwhare speaks of pohutukawa bleeding 'their short-lived brilliance';[6] Samoan Talosaga Tolovae finds, in the Waikato, 'A pohutukawa tree [that] crushes, Red into symmetrical flowers/Against the grey walls of the sky . . .';[7] artist-poet Rei Hamon salutes the gulf that is Hauraki:

> Now the tree buds have burst above.
> Such beauty, I know its worth,
> I give whispered thanks to Him whose love
> Gave me Hauraki's waters that lie beyond the Firth.[8]

Hamon seems to be the exception, in writing of the silver buds of the pohutukawa, rather than the crimson flowers.

Muriel Parker, in her collection *The Roaring Silence*, writes in *Through a Sudden Gate* of

> . . . A huge gnarled pohutukawa
> Bent with age and yet so beautiful
> Lit with the jubilation of a Christmas tree,
> Hangs her deep red branches
> Like honey-sweet wine
> Over the warm flashing blue of the summer sea.[9]

And there is Alan Mulgan's 'when pohutukawa dips, Red on our blue infinities';[10] Margaret T. South's pohutukawa 'in full bloom/Stopping the sun like giant red umbrellas';[11] and Bob Laws' pohutukawa spreading 'their welcoming carpets'.[12] Ronald Castle compared the falling of pohutukawa stamens — 'Red stamens fall like sand, Telling their own passing' — to a 'January hour-glass'.[13]

Ronald Castle's later poem *In December* celebrates New Zealand's Christmas tree:

> Now the red flowers of Pohutukawa
> Burst from the shapely blossoming trees
> Lining the streets and avenues shady,
> Flaming on beaches washed by our seas.
>
> Every mid summer, viewless to mortals,
> Lit they with fire this loneliest land,
> Even as paused o'er Bethlehem's stable
> Starlight commanded shepherds to stand
>
> Leaving their flocks unguarded on hillsides,
> Beckoned by sound of angelic choir
> Down to the couch of Joseph and Mary,
> Where lay the babe of ages' desire.

The grove of pohutukawa at the Treaty House, Waitangi, was planted by successive governors-general.

Sway to and fro your reddening burdens,
Burn unconsumed to heavenly flames;
Scatter your redness down upon mortals,
Whispering in awe that Name of all names.[14]

In *Nova Zelandiae* Barbara Hulse pays tribute to the 'one Creator' and to the trees that 'both reward and serve us well'; the pohutukawa is the only tree identified:

O beloved Pohutukawa,
Christmas tree of our fair land,
Giving warmth of colour and restful shade,
To all who work with heart and hand.

Created by the one Creator,
Trees and men in harmony dwell,
Depending both on
Providence kind.
Trees both reward and serve us well.[15]

One poet managed to pay colourful homage to the pohutukawa without mentioning the name of the tree. Anthologist, critic and poet, Allen Curnow, contributed his praise in *Spectacular Blossom* and there is no doubting the tree to which he refers as 'woody tumours burst in scarlet spray'.[16]

The full majesty of the pohutukawa outside Grey House, Wanganui Collegiate.

In another century, on the other side of the world, and in fiction, not verse, another author included the pohutukawa in his writings. The author is anonymous, but some reasoned speculation points the finger to no less a literary giant than Charles Dickens. Did the author of such loved classics as *Pickwick Papers* and *A Christmas Carol* in fact write a longish short story based on New Zealand and which referred to 'a pohutukawa, a large crooked evergreen tree found in New Zealand and bearing, about Christmas, a most beautiful crimson bloom . . .'? For good measure, he added that boatbuilders in New Zealand 'use the crooked limbs of this tree for the knees and elbows of their boats'.[17]

That Charles Dickens knew of New Zealand and might have contemplated emigrating here is confirmed in a letter he wrote to a friend in 1847, when depressed by a critical review of his Christmas book: 'Inimitable very mouldy and dull . . . Disposed to go to New Zealand and start a magazine.'[18]

This comment is quoted by editor J. S. Ryan in *Charles Dickens and New Zealand*, with notes by A. H. Reed, in which the authors speculate whether Dickens wrote *From the Black Rocks on Friday*. This story appeared first in *All the Year Round*, a weekly periodical which Dickens edited and in which much of his shorter work appeared.

The story tells of the adventures of an English clergyman shipwrecked on an uninhabited island somewhere to the north of New Zealand (perhaps in the Kermadecs group) for six months after his fishing boat was driven by a storm from the Black Rocks off the Bay of Islands and then lost:

> Unlike Robinson Crusoe, I had not even a dog or a cat for my companion, I had no wrecked ship wherefrom to draw any resources. I was totally unarmed. I had no tools wherewith to build, or plant, or dig; I had no seeds to plant even had I tools. I had no books to while away the long, tedious hours, no means whereon to write even an account of my sufferings and fate, though perchance they might one day be read in my bones whitening on the beach. I was without house or shelter, and without fire.[19]

How this castaway managed to survive, virtually an account of his day-to-day experiences, is the basis of quite a good story. Included are some Maori words, used when he is at last found. If Charles Dickens did write this story, where did he get his background information, including the Maori?

And where, the detail about the pohutukawa tree to which he attached his ill-fated boat when landing on the deserted island? The author describes his landing place (the story is told in the first person) as including

> a steep gully, narrow and blocked up with huge boulders, [down which] fell the small stream of water, trickling finally in little rills over the green slimy surface of a rock about thirty feet high. In the clefts of the rock were growing shrubs, with here and there the larger growth of a pohutukawa, a large crooked evergreen tree found in New Zealand, and bearing, about Christmas, a most beautiful crimson bloom: the boat-builders in New Zealand use the crooked limbs of this tree for the knees and elbows of their boats.[20]

The story appeared in May 1862, three years after *All the Year Round* appeared, as a more literary successor to *Household Words*. The new magazine featured in serial form *A Tale of Two Cities*, with *Great Expectations* appearing in 1860–61. In addition, Dickens about this time began the popular and celebrated readings from his works. All this made him a very busy man, but he did write shorter pieces for the magazines he edited. Did he write *From the Black Rocks on Friday*?

Here in New Zealand children's writers have generally shied away from the subject of the pohutukawa, but in the 1950s Avis Acres wrote of two appealing pohutukawa babies, Hutu and Kawa, who lived in a cosy little nest at the top of an old pohutukawa tree. All the birds and the forest folk were their friends, delightfully illustrated in these charming stories.

But, in all New Zealand literature, one man dominates the pohutukawa scene. Dramatist, critic and actor, Bruce Mason was a major figure in our theatre, his contribution recognised with such honours as a CBE and an honorary D Litt. from Victoria University. He died in 1983.

His play, *The Pohutukawa Tree*, is known to hundreds, perhaps thousands, of New Zealand schoolchildren as well as to adult theatre audiences both here and overseas. The play, a classic of New Zealand theatre, was written for production by the New Zealand Players, a brave professional company which toured the country in the 1950s.

Dominating the stage setting of the front porch of Aroha Mataira's home at a beach settlement on the Hauraki Gulf is a gnarled pohutukawa in full bloom — 'tiny red coronets pricking through the leaves.'[21] As the story unfolded in the play marches to its end, the pohutukawa sickens as if in sympathy, the branches droop, becoming 'a menace all over the porch . . .'.

It is a far time from when the tree stood so proudly a guardian sentry over the fortunes of the widow Aroha's household, as a living reminder of when the warrior Whetumarama and his followers successfully defended Te Parenga Bay against 400 soldiers ('red coats and crossed straps') from the ship of white sails, *Alcestis*. The Pakeha captain was killed by Whetumarama's taiaha, 200 soldiers were left dead and 'the great ship *Alcestis* spread its wings, borne away on the great wave of fear'.[22]

Te Parenga pa was never taken by force, but slowly ('slice by slice from the whale; by time') the land was lost by sale to the Pakeha, except for the last strip on which stood Aroha's house and the old pohutukawa, itself growing on land hallowed by blood. As Aroha recalls: '. . . this old pohutukawa. It was planted by Whetumarama himself. On the day after the battle he planted it where the pakeha captain fell, that its red flowers might be a sign of blood between Maori and pakeha for ever.'[23]

It is a play relevant to its times and even prophetic of what has happened in New Zealand since. Aroha is a fiercely dedicated Christian, as much identified with her religion as with her land, so when her only daughter becomes pregnant to a Pakeha barman (who refuses to marry her because of her race) and her only son vandalises the church at Te Parenga, she disowns both and surrenders life, by willing herself to die as her pride dictates — 'I go to my dark. To my only home.'

This is a theme, as James Bertram has said, of true tragic potential, reflecting an aspect of racial relations in a confused world.[24] Of the stage accessories, the most visible is the tree which gives the play its name.

Te Parenga, according to Bruce Mason, was Takapuna, where 'the beach is fringed with pohutukawa trees, single and stunted in the gardens, spreading and noble on the cliffs, and in the empty spaces by the foreshore. Tiny red coronets prick through the gray-green leaves. Bark, flower and leaf seem overlaid by smoke. The red is of a dying fire at dusk, the green faded and drab. Pain and age are in these gnarled forms, in bare roots, clutching at the earth, knotting on the cliff-face, in tortured branches, dark against the washed sky.' This, for Bruce Mason, was 'my heritage, my world'.[25]

Perhaps, as another poet sang, the best is yet to be and Professor Blaiklock's dream will be realised — someone will 'find this poetry of native trees' to a better measure still. This is not to deny the appeal of much that has been written in praise of the pohutukawa. Most New Zealand poets of substance have at least acknowledged the Christmas blossom, while some have accorded it a full Yuletide salute, impressed, in their turn, as were members of the Arawa canoe who saw such a fantastic crimson parade on the new shoreline.

The pohutukawa, this 'Christian tree of our fair land', should continue to inspire the poets who seek to lift hearts and hopes at a season of everlasting goodwill.

Appendix I
Description by Dr Daniel Solander

A translation from the Latin description of the pohutukawa (*Metrosideros excelsa*) by Dr Daniel Solander in the manuscript 'Primitiae Florae Novae Zelandiae sive Catalogus Plantarum in Eahelino Mauwe and Tavai Poenamimoo diebus 8 Octobris — 31 Marlii A.D. MDCCLXIX and MDCCLXX collectarum' ('Beginnings of a flora of New Zealand or a catalogue of plants collected in the North and South Islands between 8 October and 31 March 1769–1770').

Note: Where very botanical terms have been used in this translation, an explanation is provided in square brackets.

The 'pohutuiawha' of the New Zealanders.

It grows in New Zealand, near Opuragi, Totaranui.

Large *tree* with diffuse crown.

Branches almost cylindrical, dichotomous, branchlets scarcely compressed, greenish, covered with very short white matted hairs.

Leaves opposite, spreading, short stalked, elliptic, acute-tipped, with entire margins, flat, leathery, 4 inches long, upper surface deep green, smooth, shining, lower surface with very short matted hairs, whitish, much veined; *veins* numerous, thin, indistinct, parallel, running together at an obtuse angle; on the upper surface near the margin a fine nerve runs up to the tip, which is not visible on the lower surface.

Petioles [leaf-stalks] eight times shorter than the leaves, with matted hairs, slightly channelled in upper part.

Corymbs [flower-heads] terminal, paired, shorter than the leaves, usually branches in threes three times; peduncles lateral, unbranched, bearing three flowers. *Flowers* sessile.

Rachis and Peduncles [main axis and branchlets of the flower head] white with very dense short hairs.

Note: Raches and corymbs persist on the *branchlets* and grow out where branches are dichotomous; the *peduncles* often remain for two years.

Calyx monophyllous [having one leaf only], funnel-shaped, matted with white hairs, persistent; *tube* top-shaped, obtusely five-angled; *limb* five-partite; segments ovate, acute-tipped, rather spreading, shorter than the tube, ⅙ inch long.

Note: a fruit-bearing calyx becomes vase-shaped and hardened, with erect segments.

Petals five, ovate-oblong, rather obtuse, concave, with rolled-in margins, so that at first glance they seem narrow and acute-tipped; inserted on the calyx and twice as long as its teeth [calyx segments], spreading, pale reddish, on the outside becoming greyish from the base to above the middle with very short hairs. The tube of the calyx is filled with nectar at the nectar spot above the ovary.

Filaments about twenty-five, inserted on the calyx, filiform, five times longer than the petals, often 1½ inches long, erect, deep red. *Anthers* oval, small, folded inwards, dull red. *Pollen* yellow.

Ovary superior, sunk at the base of the calyx, roundish. *Style* filiform, erect, slightly longer and thicker than the stamens, pale red. Stigma unbranched, truncate.

Capsule oval, obtuse, hairy, ¼ inch long, three-locular, three-valved.

Seeds very numerous, like golden sawdust, shining.

Appendix II
Pohutukawa: *Its Botanical Status*

There are two species which in New Zealand are called pohutukawa. The first, given the botanical name *Metrosideros excelsa*, grows naturally in northern New Zealand, on the coasts from the Three Kings Islands in the far north to Urenui in Taranaki and Poverty Bay on the East Coast, as well as on lake shores in the Rotorua district. It is what is commonly known as pohutukawa.

The second, *Metrosideros kermadecensis*, known as Kermadec pohutukawa, is found naturally only on Raoul Island in the Kermadec Islands, almost 1000 kilometres north of New Zealand. Both look similar to each other and are now widely cultivated throughout the country.

M. excelsa is distinguished by the generally larger size of all its parts, and its pointed-tipped leaves. *M. kermadecensis* is somewhat smaller and more compact, with rounded-tipped leaves. Although both may be flowering at once, and at any time of the year, the peak flowering for *M. kermadecensis* is slightly earlier (around November–December) than that of *M. excelsa* (around December–January). A yellow-flowered form of *M. excelsa* was found on Motiti Island in the Bay of Plenty about 1940 and cultivars of it have become popular for planting. Variegated and other cultivars are also now available.

The closest relatives of the pohutukawa are the various varieties of *Metrosideros collina*, which grow on many islands throughout Polynesia. These look superficially almost identical to *M. excelsa* and *M. kermadecensis*. The pohutukawa are also closely related to the New Zealand rata and in fact are all placed in the same genus (*Metrosideros*):

M. albiflora, *M. colensoi*, *M. diffusa* and *M. perforata* are all white-flowered climbers.

M. carminea is a crimson-flowered climber.

M. fulgens (winter rata) is a climber with orange-scarlet (occasionally yellow) flowers.

M. parkinsonii is a crimson-flowered straggling shrub or small tree.

M. robusta (northern rata) and *M. umbellata* (southern rata) are forest trees, often huge, with scarlet flowers.

M. bartlettii, a large tree with white flowers, somehow escaped notice until 1975 and is now known from several localities in the very far north of the North Island.

The pohutukawa and rata are all within the plant family Myrtaceae. This is a large family of about 100 genera and 3000 species distributed throughout the tropics and sub-tropics, chiefly America, southern Africa, south-east Asia and Australia. It includes the myrtles, eucalypts (gums), guavas, cloves, feijoas and bottlebrushes, from which come such highly valuable products as excellent timber and a range of spices, medicines and edible fruits. In New Zealand, the family includes manuka (*Leptospermum scoparium*), kanuka (*Kunzea ericoides*), ramarama (*Lophomyrtus bullata*), rohutu (*Lophomyrtus obcordata* and *Neomyrtus pedunculata*), and maire tawaki or swamp maire (*Syzgium maire*).

Economic values of the pohutukawa are several. Their timber is extremely strong and hard and has been used in the past for ready-made curves in shipbuilding. The wood is also highly decorative and prized for carving and turning. An infusion of the inner bark was traditionally used (and sometimes still is) as a treatment for diarrhoea. Nectar from the flowers is the source of a honey valued for its special flavour and soothing effect on sore throats. The nectar is also highly attractive to native honey-eating birds and insects and fought over by them. Last but not least, pohutukawa make spectacular additions to the New Zealand natural landscape and to gardens.

For further reference:

Eagle's Trees and Shrubs of New Zealand, by Audrey Eagle. Published by Collins, 1982 (revised 1986).

The Native Trees of New Zealand, by J. T. Salmon. Published by A.H. & A.W. Reed, 1980.

Flowering Plants of the World, published by Croom Helm, 1985.

Geoff Walls
Botany Division, DSIR
Havelock North

Text References

CHAPTER 1 In the Beginning
1. F. Von Hochstetter, *New Zealand: The Physical Geography, Geology and Natural History*, J. G. Cotta, Stuttgart, 1867, p. 135.
2. A. S. Thomson, *The Story of New Zealand*, John Murray, London, 1859, p. 16.
3. *Ibid.*, p. 17.
4. F. Von Hochstetter, *op. cit.*, p. 133.
5. Eileen Duggan, *New Zealand Poems*, George Allen & Unwin, London, 1940, p. 56.
6. R. M. Laing and E. W. Blackwell, *Plants of New Zealand*, Whitcombe & Tombs, Christchurch, 1927, p. 281.
7. Ernst Dieffenbach, *Travels in New Zealand*, reprint, Capper Press, 1974, Vol. 1, p. 223.
8. Margaret T. South, *The Land of the Tattooed Faces*, Salix Press, Auckland, 1978, p. 8.
9. Elsdon Best, *Maori Religion and Mythology*, Government Printer, Wellington, 1982, p. 424.
10. Sir Peter Buck, *The Coming of the Maori*, Whitcombe & Tombs, Christchurch, 1949, p. 49.
11. Sir Peter Buck, *ibid.*, p. 50.
12. *Transactions and Proceedings of the New Zealand Institute*, Vol. XIV, p. 65.
13. Sir Peter Buck, *op. cit.*, p. 47.
14. *Ibid.*, p. 50.
15. A. H. Reed, *First New Zealand Christmasses*, A. H. & A. W. Reed, Wellington, 1933, pp. 17–19.
16. Rev. J. B. Marsden, *Memoirs of the Life and Labours of the Rev. Samuel Marsden of Parramatta*, London, 1857, p. 101.
17. Letter to author, 7 September 1986.
18. A. H. Reed, *op. cit.*, p. 21.
19. Thomas Kirk, *The Forest Flora of New Zealand*, Government Printer, Wellington, 1889, p. 241.

CHAPTER 2 Pohutukawa Pioneers
1. As resolved by Royal Society 1767, *Native Trees and Shrubs*, New Zealand Education Department, Wellington, 1947, p. 2.
2. Sir J. D. Hooker, *Journal of the Rt. Hon. Sir Joseph Banks*, Macmillan & Co., London, 1896, p. 185.
3. J. C. Beaglehole (ed.), *The Endeavour Journal of Joseph Banks 1768–1771*, Trustees of the Public Library of New South Wales, 1962, Vol. 1, p. 403.

4. J. C. Beaglehole, *The Life of Captain James Cook*, Adam & Charles Black, London, 1974, p. 201.
5. Sir J. D. Hooker, *op. cit.*, pp. 191–193.
6. *Ibid.*, p. 227.
7. *Ibid.*, p. 228.
8. *Ibid.*, p. 228.
9. *Native Trees and Shrubs*, *op. cit.*, p. 3.
10. Sir J. D. Hooker, *op. cit.*, p. xxvi.
11. *Ibid.*, p. 9.
12. Augustus Earle, *Narrative of a Residence in New Zealand: Journal of a Residence in Tristan da Cunha* (ed. E. H. McCormick), Clarendon Press, Oxford, 1966, p. 88.
13. F. Von Hochstetter, *New Zealand: The Physical Geography, Geology and Natural History*, J. G. Cotta, Stuttgart, 1867, p. 240.
14. *Ibid.*, p. 142.
15. Sir J. D. Hooker, *Handbook of New Zealand Flora*, Lovell Reeve & Co., London, 1867, p. 240.
16. G. H. Scholefield, *Dictionary of New Zealand Biography*, Government Printer, Wellington, 1940, Vol. 1, p. 470.
17. Thomas Kirk, *The Forest Flora of New Zealand*, Government Printer, Wellington, 1889, p. 11.
18. *Ibid.*, p. 237.
19. *Ibid.*, p. 238.
20. Mona Gordon, *The Garden of Tane*, A. H. & A. W. Reed, Wellington, p. 50.
21. Dr L. Cockayne and E. P. Turner, *The Trees of New Zealand*, Government Printer, Wellington, 1967, dedication.
22. *Ibid.*, p. 163.
23. *Ibid.*, p. 258.
24. Sarah and Edward Featon, *The Art Album of New Zealand Flora*, Bock & Cousins, Wellington, 1889, p. 163.
25. *Ibid.*, p. 263.
26. W. Martin, *The New Zealand Nature Book*, Whitcombe & Tombs, Wellington, 1929, Vol. 2, p. 74.

CHAPTER 3 The Foremost Botanist
1. Sir J. D. Hooker, *Handbook of New Zealand Flora*, Lovell Reeve & Co., London, 1867, p. 11.
2. *Transactions and Proceedings of the New Zealand Institute*, Vol. 1, 1868, p. 30.
3. *Ibid.*, p. 235.
4. *Ibid.*, p. 273.
5. *Ibid.*, p. 282.

6. *Ibid.*, Vol. XXVII, Government Printer, London, p. 368.
7. *Ibid.*, 1867, p. 283.

CHAPTER 4 The Sacred and the Great
1. Friends of Urban Trees (Auckland), newsletter, May 1985.
2. S. W. Burstall and E. V. Sale, *Great Trees of New Zealand*, A. H. & A. W. Reed, Wellington, 1984, p. ix.
3. *Ibid.*, p. ix.
4. Ernst Dieffenbach, *Travels in New Zealand*, reprint, Capper Press, 1974, Vol. 2, p. 384.
5. Sir Maui Pomare and James Cowan, *Legends of the Maori*, Fine Arts (NZ) Ltd, 1930, p. 252.
6. *Ibid.*, p. 253.
7. S. W. Burstall, unpublished New Zealand Forest Service data.
8. Professor H. B. Kirk, *Transactions and Proceedings of the New Zealand Institute*, 1896, Vol. XXIX, p. 512.
9. Johannes Andersen, *Maori Place Names*, Polynesian Society, Wellington, 1942, p. 78.
10. Letter to author, 20 March 1987.
11. Card sample, Harry Conway, Gisborne.
12. Sir Peter Buck, *The Coming of the Maori*, Whitcombe & Tombs, Christchurch, 1949, p. 51.
13. Muriel E. Fisher, E. Satchell and Janet M. Watkins, *Gardening with New Zealand Trees and Shrubs*, Collins, Auckland, 1970, p. 79.
14. Julian Matthews, *AA Trees in New Zealand*, Lansdowne Press/AA, Auckland, 1983, p. 66.

CHAPTER 5 The New Beginnings
1. F. Von Hochstetter, *New Zealand: The Physical Geography, Geology and Natural History*, J. G. Cotta, Stuttgart, 1867, p. 249.
2. *Ibid.*, p. 259.
3. *Ibid.*, p. 258.
4. *Ibid.*, p. 258.
5. Ernst Dieffenbach, *Travels in New Zealand*, reprint, Capper Press, 1974, Vol. 1, p. 293.
6. Sir J. Logan Campbell, *Poenamo*, Whitcombe & Tombs, Christchurch, 1952, p. 55.
7. *Ibid.*, p. 56.
8. Whangarei District Conservator John Gardiner, *New Zealand Herald*, 30 October 1987.
9. *New Zealand Herald*, 30 October 1987.
10. *Ibid.*, 20 December 1985.
11. S. W. Burstall and E. V. Sale, *Great Trees of New Zealand*, A. H. & A. W. Reed, Wellington, 1984, p. 55.

12. *New Zealand Herald*, 25 March 1978.
13. Letter to author, 25 March 1987.

CHAPTER 6 The Flowers of Spirits' Flight
1. Sir Maui Pomare and James Cowan, *Legends of the Maori*, Fine Arts (NZ) Ltd, 1930, p. 297.
2. James Baxter, *New Zealand in Colour*, A. H. & A. W. Reed, Wellington, 1961, caption to plate 1.
3. Sir Maui Pomare and James Cowan, *op. cit.*, p. 50.
4. Ernst Dieffenbach, *Travels in New Zealand*, reprint, Capper Press, 1974, Vol. 1, p. 200.
5. Sarah and Edward Featon, *The Art Album of New Zealand Flora*, Bock & Cousins, Wellington, 1889, p. 164.
6. Sir Maui Pomare and James Cowan, *op. cit.*, p. 50.
7. J. R. Elder, *Letters and Journals of Samuel Marsden 1765–1838*, Otago University Council, 1932, p. 291.
8. *Ibid.*, p. 291.
9. Edward Tregear, *The Maori Race*, A. D. Willis, Wanganui, 1926, p. 409.
10. Sir Maui Pomare and James Cowan, *op. cit.*, p. 49.
11. Edward Tregear, *op. cit.*, p. 410.
12. *Ibid.*, p. 411.
13. T. W. Gudgeon, *History and Traditions of the Maoris*, H. Brett, Auckland, 1885, p. 117.
14. Sir Maui Pomare and James Cowan, *op. cit.*, p. 51.
15. John White, *Te Rou*, Sampson Low & Searle, London, 1874, Vol. 1, p. 24.
16. *Ibid.*, p. 24.
17. *Ibid.*, p. 25.
18. Michael King, *Being Pakeha*, Hodder & Stoughton, Auckland, 1985, p. 87.
19. Edward Shortland, *Traditions and Superstitions of New Zealanders*, reprint, Capper Press, p. 152.
20. Sir Maui Pomare and James Cowan, *op. cit.*, p. 52.

CHAPTER 8 Pohutukawa and Poets
1. E. M. Blaiklock, *Green Shade*, A. H. & A. W. Reed, Wellington, 1967, p. 48.
2. *Ibid.*, p. 48.
3. Alfred Domett, *Ranolf and Amohia*, Smith Elder & Co., London, 1872, p. 474.
4. Fay Clayton, *The Tablet*, 1972 and *Song of the Trees*, 1976, Karori, Wellington, p. 15.
5. Cynthia Watson, *Poems of Today*, Brookfield Press, Auckland, 1981, p. 143.
6. Hone Tuwhare, *No Ordinary Sun*, John McIndoe, Dunedin, 1977, p. 42.

7. Talosaga Tolovae, *The Shadows Within*, Rimu Publishing, Hamilton, 1984.
8. Rei Hamon, *Oku Mahora (My Thoughts)*, Thames Star.
9. Muriel Parker, *Roaring Silence*, Brookfield Press, Auckland.
10. Alan Mulgan, *Aldebaran and Other Verses*, Caxton Press, p. 5.
11. Margaret T. South, *The Land of the Tattooed Faces*, Salix Press, Auckland, 1978, p. 8.
12. Bob Laws, *Poetry for Peanuts*, Vol. 2, p. 19.
13. Ronald B. Castle, *Fleeting Music*, Wright & Carman, Wellington, 1937.
14. Ronald B. Castle, *The Select Poetry of Ronald Castle*, Castle Publications, 1983, p. 33.
15. Barbara Hulse, *Through a Window and Other Poems*, Cambridge Independent, 1974, p. 5.
16. Allen Curnow, *Collected Poems 1933–1973*,
A. H. & A. W. Reed, Wellington, 1974, p. 193.
17. J. S. Ryan and A. H. Reed, *Charles Dickens and New Zealand*, A. H. & A. W. Reed, Wellington, 1965, p. 142.
18. *Ibid.*, p. 133.
19. *Ibid.*, p. 142.
20. *Ibid.*, p. 142.
21. Bruce Mason, *The End of the Golden Weather*, New Zealand University Press & Price Milburn, 1962, p. 85.
22. *Ibid.*, p. 31.
23. Bruce Mason, *The Pohutukawa Tree*, Victoria University Press, Wellington, 1986, p. 24.
24. James Bertram *in* James Vinson (ed.), *Contemporary Dramatists*, St James Press, London, 1973, p. 513.
25. Bruce Mason, *The End of the Golden Weather*, p. 33.

A Select Bibliography

Allan, H. H. *Flora of New Zealand*, Vol. 1, Government Printer, Wellington, 1961.

Banks, Sir Joseph. *Journal*, Macmillan, London, 1896.

Beaglehole, J. C. *The Discovery of New Zealand*, Oxford University Press, 1961.

Blaiklock, E. M. *Green Shade*, A.H. & A.W. Reed, Wellington, 1967.

Burstall, S. W. & Sale, E. V. *Great Trees of New Zealand*, A.H. & A.W. Reed, Wellington, 1984.

Cheeseman, T. F. *Manual of New Zealand Flora*, Government Printer, Wellington, 1906.

Dieffenbach, Ernst. *Travels in New Zealand*, Capper reprint, 1974.

Duggan, Eileen. *New Zealand Poems*, George Allen & Unwin, 1940.

Duncan & Davies catalogue.

Featon, Mr & Mrs E. G. *The Art Album of New Zealand Flora*, Bock & Cousins, Wellington, 1889.

Fisher, Muriel E., Satchell, E. & Watkins, Janet M. *Gardening with New Zealand Flowers and Shrubs*, Collins, 1970.

Hochstetter, Ferdinand. *New Zealand: The Physical Geography, Geology and Natural History*, J. G. Cotta, Stuttgart, 1867.

King, Michael. *Being Pakeha*, Hodder & Stoughton, Auckland, 1985.

Kirk, Thomas. *The Forest Flora of New Zealand*, Government Printer, Wellington, 1889.

Maddock, Shirley. *Islands of the Gulf*, Collins, 1966.

Marsden, Rev. J. B. (ed.) *Memoirs of the Life and Labours of the Rev. Samuel Marsden of Parramatta*, London, 1857.

Mason, Bruce. *The Pohutukawa Tree*, Victoria University Press, Wellington, 1986.

Pomare, Hon. Sir Maui & Cowan, James. *Legends of the Maori*, Fine Arts (NZ), 1930.

Reed, A. H. *Farthest North: Afoot in Maoriland Byways*, A.H. & A.W. Reed, 1946.

Reed, A. H. *First New Zealand Christmasses*, A.H. & A.W. Reed, 1933.

Stafford, D. M. *Te Arawa: A History of the Arawa People*, A.H. & A.W. Reed, 1967.

Tregear, Edward. *The Maori Race*, A. D. Willis, Wanganui, 1926.

Journal of the Polynesian Society.

Transactions and Proceedings of the New Zealand Institute.

Index

Figures in italics refer to illustrations.

GEOFF CONLY was a daily newspaper journalist all his working life. He began as a copy boy on the *Dunedin Evening Star* and was deputy chief-of-staff there when appointed associate editor of the *Taranaki Herald* in 1951. He was editor of the *Napier Daily Telegraph* from 1960 until his retirement in 1978. In semi-retirement he has written several books, the best known being *The Shock of '31*, *Tarawera: The Destruction of the Pink and White Terraces* and *Piet's Eye in the Sky*.

MAURICE CONLY began his art training in Dunedin and, following his involvement in the printing and advertising industries, has been an independent artist for many years. As official artist of the Royal New Zealand Air Force, he has travelled widely in New Zealand and the Pacific, and his paintings are featured in the RNZAF history, *Portrait of an Air Force*. Two tours to the Antarctic led to the publication of *Ice on my Palette*, in collaboration with author Neville Peat. He is also widely known as a coin and stamp designer.

Other Grantham House Books

A NEW ZEALAND GUIDE TO MINIATURE ROSES
Margaret Hayward

Over 330 colour plates including a colour illustrated dictionary of miniature roses available in New Zealand.

THE NEW ZEALAND EUROPEAN CONNECTION
Martin O'Connor

An interesting insight for anyone planning a visit to Europe. The author travelled to 22 European centres which have special links with New Zealand.

THE COLONIAL NEW ZEALAND WARS
Tim Ryan and Bill Parham

An illustrated military history of the campaigns, personalities, weapons and uniforms. Over 300 photographs, drawings and paintings.

THE FOUR-LEGGED MAJOR
Graham Spencer   *Illustrated by Peter McIntyre*

A poignant, compelling story about a bull terrier dog that went to war with the New Zealand Army.

WHEN TRAMS WERE TRUMPS IN NEW ZEALAND
Graham Stewart

Suburban travel before the motorcar. New Zealanders rode them to school, to work, to sports and many to fame. A pictorial parade through the changing facades of our cities.

THE HARBOUR FERRIES OF AUCKLAND
David Balderston

The special delight of a ferry trip on Auckland Harbour. From the grand old Victorian and Edwardian ladies of the early ferry companies to the vessels used today.

RAIL — The Great New Zealand Adventure
Roy Sinclair

A comprehensive illustrated volume with over 100 colour plates. The journeys through rugged landscape and alpine regions interwoven with anecdotes — the poets, the pioneers.

THE KID FROM MATATA
David McGill

Growing up in a small, sleepy rural community just after the Second World War. A postwar Pakeha childhood of hard yakker and simple pleasures.

PORTRAIT OF AN AIR FORCE
The Royal New Zealand Air Force
Geoffrey Bentley and Maurice Conly

A celebration of RNZAF aircraft, squadrons and personnel — a timely tribute to our Air Force. 28 full-colour oil paintings, 73 charcoal drawings and over 200 photographs.

Savour the Word
THE LANGUAGE OF ALCOHOL
Fay Clayton   *Illustrated by Caroline Campbell*

A toast to the English language. A fascinating journey through the history and meanings of the language of alcohol.